The Compl[ete Guide]
for CISA Examination
Preparation

Internal Audit and IT Audit

Series Editor

Dan Swanson, Dan Swanson and Associates, Ltd.,
Winnipeg, Manitoba, Canada.

The Internal Audit and IT Audit series publishes leading-edge books on critical subjects facing audit executives as well as internal and IT audit practitioners. Key topics include Audit Leadership, Cybersecurity, Strategic Risk Management, Auditing Various IT Activities and Processes, Audit Management, and Operational Auditing.

The Complete Guide for CISA Examination Preparation
Richard E. Cascarino

Blockchain for Cybersecurity and Privacy: *Architectures, Challenges, and Applications*
Yassine Maleh, Mohammad Shojafar, Mamoun Alazab, Imed Romdhani

The Cybersecurity Body of Knowledge: *The ACM/IEEE/AIS/IFIP Recommendations for a Complete Curriculum in Cybersecurity*
Daniel Shoemaker, Anne Kohnke, Ken Sigler

Corporate Governance: *A Pragmatic Guide for Auditors, Directors, Investors, and Accountants*
Vasant Raval

The Audit Value Factor
Daniel Samson

Managing IoT Systems for Institutions and Cities
Chuck Benson

Fraud Auditing Using CAATT: *A Manual for Auditors and Forensic Accountants to Detect Organizational Fraud*
Shaun Aghili

How to Build a Cyber-Resilient Organization
Dan Shoemaker, Anne Kohnke, Ken Sigler

Auditor Essentials: *100 Concepts, Tips, Tools, and Techniques for Success*
Hernan Murdock

Project Management Capability Assessment: *Performing ISO 33000-Based Capability Assessments of Project Management*
Peter T. Davis, Barry D. Lewis

For more information about this series please visit: https://www.routledge.com/Internal-Audit-and-IT-Audit/book-series/CRCINTAUDITA

The Complete Guide
for CISA Examination
Preparation

Richard E. Cascarino

CRC Press
Taylor & Francis Group
AN AUERBACH BOOK

First edition published 2021
by CRC Press
6000 Broken Sound Parkway NW, Suite 300, Boca Raton, FL 33487-2742

and by CRC Press
2 Park Square, Milton Park, Abingdon, Oxon, OX14 4RN

ISBN: 9781138308763 (hbk)
ISBN: 9780367551742 (pbk)
ISBN: 9780429030000 (ebk)

Typeset in Caslon Pro
by Deanta Global Publishing Services, Chennai, India

Contents

The Complete Guide for CISA Examination Preparation

Introduction

For any organization to survive and compete successfully in today's environment, successful implementation of appropriate Computer Systems is essential. Such implementation involves not only the development of appropriate systems, but also their usage, maintenance, and reliability. Protection of information assets, systems availability, data integrity, confidentiality, and robustness have become non-negotiables in the competitive world we face today.

In response to this, ISACA has updated its Certified Information Systems Auditor (CISA) certification as of June 2019 to reflect the changing priorities and industry trend in order to ensure the alignment of the Information Systems Auditor's knowledge base with the needs of tomorrow's digital age.

In order for organizations to utilize the leverage achievable with the effective use of IT, it is important that the systems can be relied upon and they require that the auditors confirm that this is indeed the case. The modern auditors therefore require significantly more knowledge of IT, IT risk, and IT control than did their predecessors.

Today's IT systems process data in high volumes and at high speed with limited or no manual interventions and control opportunities. As a result, the control opportunities previously monitored by management have migrated within the IT environment itself. Fundamental business controls previously relied upon by the auditor, such as segregation of duties and management authorization are no longer carried out external to the IT environment and must be audited in a different manner.

The concentration of risk resulting from the shift and control implementation means that the balance between preventative, detective, and corrective controls has also had to move into alignment while technology such as cloud-based systems has moved the basis of legal constraints and burdens of proof in the event of dispute into a whole new arena.

While this may sound negative, these changes can greatly increase opportunities for auditors to deliver quality service because a concentration of risk facilitates the auditors focusing their efforts and utilizing the computer itself to assist in the audit of the IT environment and application systems usage. In addition, built-in program procedures allow the auditor to adopt a systems approach to auditing because the computer encourages consistent execution of controls as opposed to the older manual controls where execution was, to a large extent, at the mercy of the individual supervisor or manager.

The effect on the audit is that the focus can be on the control environment, its design and implementation and the substantive testing of the results of individual transactions can be significantly reduced.

Controls with IT systems may be generally classified into two main subdivisions, namely:

- **General controls** – that is, controls governing the environment within which the computer system is developed, maintained, and operated and within which the application controls operate. These controls include the implementation of appropriate systems development standards, controls over the operation of the computer installation and those governing the functioning and maintenance of System Software. As such, they have a pervasive effect on all application systems.

- **Application controls** – these are the controls which operate within the business application to ensure that data is processed completely, accurately, and in a timely manner.

Ultimately, the auditors' job is to determine if the application systems function as intended and evaluate management controls to ensure the integrity, accuracy, and completeness of all information processing.

Not only must management rely upon the work done by the auditors, whether internal or external, but they need assurance that the work is carried out to internationally accepted standards and the audit processes themselves can be relied upon. As such, management seeks independent proof that the work carried out by the auditors meets this standard.

The international standard by which IT auditors are judged is the possession of the qualification of Certified Information Systems Auditor (CISA). This designation is awarded by the Information Systems Audit and Control Association (ISACA) based upon demonstrable work experience as well as success in the CISA examination. ISACA, itself, can trace its roots to the EDP Auditors Association (EDPAA) which was founded in 1969. In 1994 it changed its name to the Information Systems Audit and Control Association and in 2008 rebranded itself as simply ISACA. Today, ISACA consists of more than 145,000 members of whom 140,000 have achieved the CISA qualification since its inception in 1978. This examination evaluates the auditors' knowledge, skills, and expertise in assessing the risks inherent within the specific IT environment and the adequacy and effectiveness of the controls implemented by management.

This book is intended as a study guide for the Certified Information Systems Auditor (CISA) examination and will consist of in-depth explanations of each topic covered within this examination as well as practice questions and tips to highlight key examination information. Each chapter will contain a summary which will serve as a quick review guide, combined with end-of-chapter questions and hands-on exercises. An examination simulation is included to get candidates familiar with the examination structures.

CISA is the most recognized certification in the world for information systems auditors and is recognized by all members of the

World Trade Organization including more than 150 governments worldwide.

The qualification is intended to affirm:

- The auditors' experience and knowledge
- The level of knowledge and competency which may be expected of the qualification holder
- The currency of the holder's knowledge due to the requirements for continuing education

From an employer's perspective it demonstrates that their IT auditor may be relied upon as a proficient and experienced professional with competencies in all five of the domains covered including:

- The Process of Auditing Information Systems
- Governance and Management of IT
- Information Systems Acquisition Development and Implementation
- Information Systems Operations, Maintenance, and Service Management
- Protection of Information Assets

while at the same time maintaining an up-to-date level of knowledge which can be relied upon as an indicator of the anticipated job performance level.

From an individual auditor's perspective, the CISA is internationally recognized as a gold standard of IT auditing professionalism. It enhances the acceptability of opinions expressed in the eyes of management and, in general, makes the auditor more marketable for future career opportunities. The auditor can also gain respect from their peers and other technical specialists. For non-specialist auditors who wish to enter the IT auditing specialization, either within the organization or as external consultants, CISA provides a recognized entrance into the booming market of IT auditing. For auditors who wish simply to understand the increasing complexities and risk elements of today's business environment, understanding the CISA dimensions will assist in the demystification of current and future control complexities.

The book is comprised of seven chapters.

- **Chapter 1** covers the CISA examination itself

- **Chapter 2** covers Domain 1 – The Process of Auditing Information Systems
- **Chapter 3** covers Domain 2 – Governance and Management of IT
- **Chapter 4** covers Domain 3 – Information Systems Acquisition, Development, and Implementation
- **Chapter 5** covers Domain 4 – Information Systems Operations, Maintenance, and Service Management
- **Chapter 6** covers Domain 5 – Protection of Information Assets
- **Chapter 7** covers preparing for the examination
- **Appendix A** contains a glossary of commonly used computer terms
- **Appendix B** contains 175 CISA-type questions from which the candidate can construct multiple simulated examinations
- **Appendix C** contains multiple choice answers to the Appendix B questions

1

INTRODUCTION TO THE CISA EXAMINATION

By the end of this chapter, readers will understand:

- The structure of the CISA examination
- The process of becoming certified
- Requirements for examination participation
- The CISA Domains
- The role of ISACA's Code of Professional Ethics
- The use and implementation ISACA Standards
- The need for maintaining continuing professional competency

The Examination Itself

The examination was revised in 2019 and consists of 150 multiple-choice questions to be answered over a four-hour period.

The examinations themselves are administered at CBT (Computer Based Testing) locations. The worldwide list of examination sites may be found at https://isacaavailability.psiexams.com/. Due to the variability of examination sites, all prospective candidates should check this list prior to registering and submitting payment for the examination since registration fees are non-refundable.

Becoming Certified

There is a four-stage process involved in becoming CISA certified.

1. **Check the Examination Schedule**

    Before candidates register and pay their fee, it is critical that they verify there is a test site available in a location the candidate can easily access. Candidates may search by location and date on the ISACA website to ensure that they can take their examination as planned.

2. Register for the Examination

Once candidates have verified that there is a suitable testing site available where and when they need it, the candidate can register for their examination. Scheduling for the examination is Step 4.

3. Pay for the Examination

Payment is required before a candidate can schedule their examination, however it is not required that payment is made at the time of registration. Candidates may pay on registering for CISA, or choose to register, study at their own pace, and pay at a later stage, prior to examination scheduling.

4. Schedule the Examination

Once site availability has been assured, registration and payment made, candidates can schedule their examination. The actual scheduling is managed on the testing partner's website, not on ISACA.org.

Experience Requirements

It is not an essential to have sufficient experience to undertake the CISA examination but in order to be classified as a full CISA, candidates are required to have five (5) or more years of experience in professional information systems auditing, control, or security work experience. In addition, there is a time limit on application. Starting from the date of initially passing the examination (not the date of original registration for the examination), a completed CISA application must be submitted to ISACA. If this is not submitted within five years from the passing date of the examination, the individual will be required to re-take and re-pass the examination.

Individual experience claimed is required to have been gained within the ten-year period preceding the application date for certification or within five years of passing the examination and must be verified independently by employers.

Educational Waivers

Individuals registering as CISAs may request waivers for a maximum of three (3) years substitution for actual IT audit experience. Educational waivers may, at ISACA's discretion, be permitted to substitute for up to two years of experience. At the time of writing, these educational substitutions may be credited.

- One year of information systems OR one year of non-IS auditing experience can be substituted for one year of experience.
- 60 to 120 credit hours (two-year or four-year degree) from university – one or two years credit respectively.
- A master's degree in information security or information technology from an accredited university – one-year credit.
- A bachelor's or master's degree from a university that enforces the ISACA-sponsored Model Curricula – one-year credit, although only where the three years of educational waiver and experience substitution have not already been claimed.
- A candidate who has obtained other degrees, qualifications, and credentials with significant IS auditing, control, assurance, or security components may submit the case to the CISA Certification Committee for consideration.

Passing the Examination

It is not uncommon for highly skilled IS auditors to fail the CISA examination at the first attempt. Generally, this is not due to a lack of knowledge, but the wrong approach to the examination as a whole and the questions in particular, which cause these problems.

CISA candidates are expected to have a broad knowledge of the overall concepts and practice of information technology within an organization as well as:

- IS risks.
- The use of controls to mitigate risks.
- The use of the appropriate security features and controls within IS components.
- The roles of the auditor in conducting IS audits, including:
  - Developing an understanding of the risks inherent within the systems as implemented.
  - Understanding the security risks within the specific architecture utilized by the organization.
  - Identification and evaluation of the controls implemented to mitigate these risks.
  - Quantify weaknesses uncovered and make appropriate recommendations to mitigate these weaknesses and improve the overall control effectiveness.

CISA Job Practice Domains and Task and Knowledge Statements

Job Practice serves as the basis for the CISA exam and indicates the knowledge requirements which are expected to be at the fingertips of all professional IS auditors to earn the certification. The CISA examination covers five Domains which encompass knowledge of:

- Domain 1 – The Process of Auditing Information Systems.
    - This domain defines the procedures and methodology that an IS auditor should follow when conducting an information systems audit.
- Domain 2 – Governance and Management of IT.
    - This domain is focused on both the leadership and organizational processes which ensure that IT operates effectively with the auditor ensuring that the organization is following its own processes and procedures.
- Domain 3 – Information Systems Acquisition, Development, and Implementation.
    - The main focus is on the auditor's role in review and validation of the acquisition and testing methods of hardware acquisition to ensure that they are both adequate and follow industry best practice, and ensuring that systems promulgated by IT are both reliable and achieve the organizational objectives.
- Domain 4 – Information Systems Operations, Maintenance, and Service Management.
    - This domain encompasses the day-to-day operations of the application systems utilized within the organization as well as the maintenance of such systems. Operations include continuity planning as well as disaster recovery planning.
- Domain 5 – Protection of Information Assets.
    - This domain has gained increasing importance over recent years and involves the review and evaluation of the internal controls intended to ensure that information systems are adequately protected against a variety of threats. From

time to time the percentage of the examination allocated to each domain may be varied by ISACA but at the time of writing are:

- Domain 1 – 21%
- Domain 2 – 16%
- Domain 3 – 18%
- Domain 4 – 20%
- Domain 5 – 25%

Additional questions may appear as IS knowledge requirements develop.

For each of these Domains, ISACA provides the CISA candidate with a list of *Task Statements* indicating the tasks a professional IS auditor may be expected to undertake and *Knowledge Statements* indicating the knowledge a CISA is expected to have available in order to professionally undertake the Domain's task list. These are covered in more detail under each Domain while, at any time, the latest list of these may be downloaded from the ISACA website at http://www.isaca.org/Certification/CISA-Certified-Information -Systems-Auditor/Job-Practice-Areas/Pages/CISA-Job-Practice -Areas.aspx.

ISACA's Code of Professional Ethics

All CISA and ISACA members are required to comply with the ISACA Code of Professional Ethics. This code is intended to guide both the professional and the personal conduct of members of ISACA as well as holders of the CISA designation. The Code states that Members and ISACA certification holders shall:

1. Support the implementation of, and encourage compliance with, appropriate standards and procedures for the effective governance and management of enterprise information systems and technology, including: audit, control, security, and risk management.
2. Perform their duties with objectivity, due diligence and professional care, in accordance with professional standards.

3. Serve in the interest of stakeholders in a lawful manner, while maintaining high standards of conduct and character, and not discrediting their profession or the Association.

4. Maintain the privacy and confidentiality of information obtained in the course of their activities unless disclosure is required by legal authority. Such information shall not be used for personal benefit or released to inappropriate parties.

5. Maintain competency in their respective fields and agree to undertake only those activities they can reasonably expect to complete with the necessary skills, knowledge, and competence.

6. Inform appropriate parties of the results of work performed including the disclosure of all significant facts known to them that, if not disclosed, may distort the reporting of the results.

7. Support the professional education of stakeholders in enhancing their understanding of the governance and management of enterprise information systems and technology, including audit, control, security, and risk management.*

Failure to comply with this Code of Professional Ethics can result in disciplinary measures being instituted against the CISA or member should an investigation into a member's or CISA's conduct deem that an infringement has taken place.

The ISACA Standards

As with all Professional Associations, ISACA has promulgated its *Standards for IS Audit and Assurance* to contain statements of mandatory requirements for IS audit and assurance.

The Standards cover:

1001 Audit Charter
1002 Organizational Independence
1003 Professional Independence
1004 Reasonable Expectation
1005 Due Professional Care
1006 Proficiency

---

* https://www.isaca.org/Certification/Code-of-Professional-Ethics/Pages/default.aspx

1007 Assertions

1008 Criteria

1201 Engagement Planning

1202 Risk Assessment in Planning

1203 Performance and Supervision

1204 Materiality

1205 Evidence

1206 Using the Work of Other Experts

1207 Irregularity and Illegal Acts

1401 Reporting

1402 Follow-Up Activities.

The latest Standards may be found at: http://www.isaca.org/Know
ledge-Center/ITAF-IS-Assurance-Audit-/IS-Audit-and-Assurance/
Pages/Standards-for-IT-Audit-and-Assurance.aspx.

Overall, the Standards are intended to indicate to IS audit and
assurance professionals the minimum acceptable level of performance
required to ensure the professional responsibilities set out in the
ISACA are met. They indicate to management the profession's expectations concerning the work of IS audit practitioners and therefore the
degree of professionalism management may expect. These Standards
are mandatory for all holders of the CISA designation.

Continuous Professional Education (CPE)

In order to ensure that all CISAs maintain an adequate level of current knowledge and proficiency in their professional field of information systems audit, control, and security, ISACA requires that, over
an annual and three-year certification period, CISAs must comply
with the following CPE requirements in order to retain validity of
their certification. CISAs must:

- Attain and report an annual minimum of twenty (20) CPE
  hours. These hours must be appropriate to the currency or
  advancement of the CISA's knowledge or ability to perform
  CISA-related tasks. The use of these hours towards meeting
  the CPE requirements for multiple ISACA certifications is
  permissible when the professional activity is applicable to satisfying the job-related knowledge of each certification.

- Submit annual CPE maintenance fees to ISACA international headquarters in full.
- Attain and report a minimum of one hundred and twenty (120) CPE hours for a three-year reporting period.
- Respond and submit required documentation of CPE activities if selected for the annual audit.
- Comply with ISACA's Code of Professional Ethics.
- Abide by ISACA's IT auditing standards.[*]

---

[*] https://www.isaca.org/Certification/CISA-Certified-Information-Systems-Audi tor/Pages/Maintain-Your-CISA.aspx

2

DOMAIN 1 – THE PROCESS OF AUDITING INFORMATION SYSTEMS

This chapter covers the processes involved in the auditing of Information Systems and the areas covered within the CISA examination. As has been noted, this domain currently approximates 21% of the examination, that is some 32 questions. Five task statements and 11 knowledge statements are included within this domain.

By the end of this chapter, readers will be able to:

- Demonstrate a knowledge of ISACA IT Audit and Assurance Standards, Guidelines and Tools and Techniques, Code of Professional Ethics, and other applicable standards.
- Understand the concepts requiring a knowledge of fundamental business processes (e.g. purchasing, payroll, accounts payable, accounts receivable) and the role of IS in these processes.
- Comprehend the control principles related to controls in information systems.
- Explain the concepts of risk-based audit planning and audit project management techniques, including follow-up.
- Explain the role of auditor understanding of the applicable laws and regulations that affect the scope, evidence collection and preservation, and frequency of audits.
- Describe the evidence collection techniques (e.g. observation, inquiry, inspection, interview, data analysis, forensic investigation techniques, computer-assisted audit.

The First Task

The first task involves the execution of an appropriate IS audit risk-based strategy in order to ensure that areas of primary risk are fully audited.

Those risk areas would be the ones with the highest impact or exposure to the organization. Such areas are typically to be found around mission-critical activities of the organization. The IS auditor must always bear in mind that not everything needs to be audited nor, indeed, can be audited and therefore areas of higher interest must be prioritized. In achieving this, the IS auditor must be cognizant of the audit strategies and standards in effect. From a CISA perspective, perhaps the best source is the Professional Practices Framework for IS Audit and Assurance (ITAF) which is downloadable from http://www.isaca.org. Although examination questions are not directly drawn from ITAF, nevertheless it covers all of the standards and guidelines incorporated within the CISA examination.

The Second Task

> The second task incorporated within this domain is that of formulating the audit plans for specific audits to determine whether information systems are protected, controlled, and provide value to the organization.

The plan incorporates the scope of the audit, i.e. what is included and what is excluded from this particular audit with the selection of systems to be audited being derived from the audit risk evaluation. The typical audit plan will include identification of system risks, internal controls designed to mitigate against those risks including both general controls, and the systems environment as well as systems-specific controls were designed to address risks within a given business application area. Having identified the governing controls, the auditor would typically identify those key controls which govern the majority of the risk and design the appropriate tests in order to evaluate the effectiveness and efficiency of these controls in mitigating the risk. The first step in designing the audit program is to identify the source of evidence which the auditor will rely on in the control evaluation. Once the evidence has been located, the auditor can select the appropriate audit technique to obtain the evidence and, if necessary, select the appropriate audit tool. The selection of such tools and techniques should be in line with the Professional Standards which, as previously indicated, may be found on the ISACA website together with guidelines, tools, and techniques for the assistance of the auditor in implementing the plan.

The Third Task

> The third task involves the execution of the audit to ensure they are
> conducted in accordance with IS audit standards to achieve planned
> audit objectives.

If the audit program designed addresses the major significant risks
and the audit tests have been designed appropriately to obtain the
desired evidence, all the auditor needs to do is follow the audit
program, obtain the evidence, and evaluate the results. The evaluation should result in a conclusion that control is being maintained
at an adequate level to mitigate the corporate risk or that it is not at
an adequate level and recommendations to improve control effectiveness will be required. Such recommendations could involve
improving the effectiveness of existing controls or, where a gap
exists in the control structure, implementation of a new control
may be required.

The Fourth Task

> Once the audit fieldwork has been completed and the results evaluated,
> the fourth task involves the communication of the audit results and rec-
> ommendations to key stakeholders and decision makers through meet-
> ings and the production of audit reports to promote change to control
> structures when necessary.

The value the organization derives from an audit depends on the
effectiveness of the communication of the results of the audit.

Typically, this will involve a presentation to executive management
of the major risks, control objectives, control effectiveness, possible
weaknesses, and recommendations for improvements. This presentation will normally be accompanied by the written audit report
which will contain an executive summary as well as detailed findings and recommendations for implementation by middle management, together with the degree of acceptance of the recommendations
and the timescale for implementation. The report should include (at
a minimum) the audit scope and objectives, a description of the audit
subject, a narrative of the audit work activity performed, conclusions,

findings, and recommendations. To be effective, audit reports must be timely, credible, readable, and have a constructive tone.

The Final Stage

> The final stage of the audit is the conducting of a follow-up. It is critical that any recommendations made within the audit report be followed up in order to determine whether management has taken the appropriate remedial steps to resolve any control weakness in a timely manner.

Occasionally the auditor may find that management has accepted the risk of taking no further action or even that management has taken no action and left the weakness as an unacceptable risk.

This follow-up will itself result in the production of report, albeit a short report, which will hopefully state that all outstanding issues have now been resolved.

Knowledge Statements

Knowledge statements describe in detail the areas and depth of knowledge the auditor requires to successfully carry out the tasks within a specific practice area.

The knowledge statements in Domain 1 cover:

Knowledge of ISACA IT Audit and Assurance Standards, Guidelines and Tools and Techniques, Code of Professional Ethics, and Other Applicable Standards

Although candidates are expected to have knowledge of both the standards and the code of professional ethics, questions are not typically drawn directly from these but rather require the auditor to interpret a question in terms of both the standards and the code of ethics and apply both in their answers.

Standards themselves are structured such that:

The 1000 series (i.e. standards 1000 to 1008) focus on the audit planning and cover:

- 1001 The Audit Charter
  - Charters tend to be common in approach although individual charters are tailored to meet the unique needs of

the organization for which they are designed. Because of its role, to define the relationship and responsibilities that should exist between the Chief Executive, the head of IS Audit, and the line audit committee. In most organizations, it is commonly perceived to be the defining terms of reference for the head of the audit function and provides top management with a measurement of the level of assurance regarding the reliability and quality of internal control within the organization. It also acts as a point of reference when the audit function's structure, plans, or reports are being reviewed.

- To the operational managers of an organization, the charter indicates the level of authority to act delegated to the audit function in reviewing each of their systems of internal control over the computer and manual systems. They may expect to see constraints within the body of the document, which preserves their own rights as decision makers.

- The form, content, and wording of the charter will normally be selected by the audit function itself. These will typically be influenced by IS Audit standards and should encourage best professional practice as defined by the appropriate professional bodies. The IS Audit charter may be an independent publication or, in the case of a formerly constituted IS Audit function, be part of the IS Audit charter.

- The document is normally signed off by both the Chief Executive and the Chairman of the Audit Committee. The document itself would typically consist of a formal definition of IS Audit within the organization and its key objectives, the authority under which the head of IS Audit acts, including the line of reporting as well as rights of access to people, properties, assets, and records, and the terms of reference describing, in detail, the role and working objectives of the head of IS Audit.

- 1002 Organizational Independence
  - The audit function must be free of any bias or influence if the integrity of the audit process is to be valued and

recognized for its contribution to the organization's goals and objectives using the appropriate reporting structures. In gathering evidence, auditors must ensure that they maintain an independent and objective attitude both in fact and in appearance. Such independence is normally taken to be in jeopardy when an auditor is charged with auditing an area where there has been line responsibility within the previous year. Many auditors interpret this as indicating that they cannot be too detailed in making recommendations because this would preclude their conducting subsequent audits due to a perceived lack of independence and objectivity. This may indeed be the case, and both management and auditors must understand that, where detailed assistance is given in designing audit implementing control structures, the auditor is functioning primarily as an internal control consultant. Subsequent auditing of these structures should be done independently of the consultant.

- 1003 Professional Independence
  - ISACA states that 'IS audit and assurance professionals shall be independent and objective in both attitude and appearance in all matters related to audit and assurance engagements'.[*]
  - This refers to the auditor's need to ensure that all engagements are carried out in an unbiased frame of mind addressing issues with impartiality both in fact and an appearance. Where any impediment, such as the assumption of non-audit roles within non-IS, exists to such independence it must be disclosed to management.
- 1004 Reasonable Expectation
  - This standard addresses the management expectations for the work done by IS audit to ensure that engagements are only undertaken if the work can be reasonably expected to be professionally accomplished against the appropriate criteria.
  - Part of this expectation will be dictated by the scope of the audit. Limitations on the scope may preclude an

---

[*] http://www.isaca.org/Knowledge-Center/Standards/Documents/1003-Professional-Independence.pdf Statement 1003.1

expression of an appropriate audit opinion on the 80 under review.

- 1005 Due Professional Care
  - This standard indicates the degree of integrity and care required of the IS auditor in conducting assignments and includes the degree of professional skepticism required during the course of the engagement. From an examination perspective, it should be noted that Due Professional Care does not require infallibility on the part of the IS auditor, only reasonable care and competence.
- 1006 Proficiency
  - The Proficiency standard addresses the professional competence required of the IS auditor in executing an assignment. This does not mean that the individual auditor must be an expert in all things, but rather that the auditor, in conjunction with others involved in the assignment should have appropriate and adequate knowledge of the area under review and a professional competence shall be maintained through appropriate continuing professional education.
- 1007 Assertions
  - Assertions are defined by ISACA as being 'any formal declaration or set of declarations about the subject matter made by management'* and this standard clarifies the need for the IS auditor to determine whether management secessions are capable of being audited as well as whether they are sufficient, relevant, and valid.
- 1008 Criteria
  - The Criteria standard spells out the manner in which the IS auditor shall select the criteria against which assessment will be made to ensure that the source of the criteria is appropriate and the criteria themselves may be seen to be:
    - Objective
    - Complete
    - Relevant

---

* http://www.isaca.org/Knowledge-Center/ITAF-IS-Assurance-Audit-/IS-Audit -and-Assurance/Pages/IS-Audit-and-Assurance-Standard-1007-Assertions.aspx

- Measurable
- Widely recognized
- Authoritative
- Understandable

The 1200 series (i.e. standards 1200 to 1208) focuses on the overall conduct of the assignment and aspects such as:

- 1201 Engagement Planning
  - To ensure adequacy of the objectives, scope, deliverables, and timeline in order to ensure compliance with both professional auditing standards and applicable laws.
  - Within this standard, ISACA stresses the use of a risk-based approach where appropriate. The plan itself should be cognizant of the nature of the engagement as well as the objectives and resource requirements needed to complete the engagement in an acceptable time scale.
- 1202 Risk Assessment in Planning
  - ISACA requires the IS auditor to use an *appropriate* risk assessment approach in developing the IS audit plan. The specific methodology to be utilized is not spelled out by the risks to the enterprise inherent in the subject matter as well as the audit risk should be covered.
- 1203 Performance and Supervision
  - It is within this standard that the management of the assignment is addressed and many CISA questions originate within the task performance and management arena.
  - Supervision is required to be carried out to ensure achievement of the audit objectives as well as to ensure the work meets the appropriate professional audit standards.
  - Within this standard, the requirement exists that evidence obtained shall be sufficient and appropriate to achieve the overall audit objectives and that the appropriate analysis has been carried out and interpreted to support the audit findings and conclusions.
  - The documentation of the audit process is also laid down as a requirement in order to ensure that findings and conclusions are appropriately supported.

- 1204 Materiality
  - Within any audit, auditors are liable to come across indications of areas for potential improvement. These may come about as a result of absence of controls or weaknesses in existing controls and the auditor must make an assessment as to whether failure in this area could potentially result in a material weakness and reduce the probability of achieving the overall business objectives of the area under review.
  - While individual weaknesses may not be classed as material, the cumulative impact may lead to significant deficiencies and would have to be judged against the overall risk evaluation. In any event, auditors will be required to disclose:
  - Control deficiencies, whether due to ineffective controls or the absence of control
  - The significance of any control deficiencies uncovered
  - The probability of individual weaknesses leading to material deficiencies
- 1205 Evidence
  - This standard relates to the appropriateness and sufficiency of evidence gathered to facilitate the drawing of reasonable conclusions and the auditor's evaluation of such sufficiency.
- 1206 Using the Work of Other Experts
  - As previously stated, the auditor is not expected to be an expert in all fields but, when the auditor encounters circumstances beyond their level of expertise, the use of other experts should be considered within the assignment. It is up to the auditor to assess and approve the adequacy of the other experts' professional competence, qualifications, experience, and independence prior to their selection and to ensure ongoing quality assurance is maintained throughout the engagement.
  - This quality assurance will involve the ongoing assessment and evaluation of the work carried out by the other experts and a conclusion on the extent to which the auditor can rely on their work.

- Where the work carried out by the external expert is deemed to be insufficient or incomplete, the IS auditor is required to apply additional techniques in order to obtain evidence that is sufficient to support the audit findings.
- It is at the auditor's discretion whether the use of such external experts is independently reported or incorporated within the overall audit report. Should the evidence found be of a limiting impact on the scope of the assignment, this must be disclosed.
- 1207 Irregularity and Illegal Acts
  - Throughout the course of any assignment, IS auditors must remain mindful of the possibility of irregularities or illegal acts. As such, professional skepticism regarding any assertions or evidence found is part and parcel of all IS audit engagements.
  - Where any such discrepancies or indications of illegality or irregularities are discovered they must be communicated to the appropriate authorities, internally or externally, in an appropriate timescale.

The 1400 series (i.e. standards 1401 to 1402) focuses on the communication of results and the information communicated including verbal and written reports in a variety of formats. Such communication can make or break the effectiveness of an audit and is a frequent source for CISA questions.

- 1401 Reporting
  - This standard specifies the need to produce a formal report at minimum at the end of an engagement, supported by sufficient and appropriate evidence. The report itself should include:
  - The identification of the enterprise reviewed as well as the intended recipients of the report and any restrictions on the report circulation all contents for individual audiences.
  - The scope of the report as well as the engagement objectives, timescale for coverage, the nature of the work undertaken, and tests conducted.
  - Audit findings, conclusions, and recommendations must be spelled out in a clear and unambiguous manner so

that the recipient of the report can clearly understand the materiality and urgency of any recommendations made.

- It is at this stage that any limitations in the scope or any qualifications regarding the findings must be spelled out by the IS auditor.
- As with all such communications, the audit report must be signed and dated according to the terms of the audit charter with the distribution as laid down in the engagement letter.

- 1402 Follow-Up Activities
  - It is critical that any recommendations made within the audit report are followed up in order to determine whether management has accepted the risk of taking no further action, taken the appropriate remedial steps to resolve any control weakness, or taken no action and left the weakness as an unacceptable risk.
  - This follow-up will itself result in the production of a report, albeit a short report, which will hopefully state that all outstanding issues have now been resolved.

Understanding the Fundamental Business Processes

Auditors must consider the impact of the audit and the overall business operations of the organization in terms of its purpose, business objectives, industry-specific regulations, business cycles, reporting cycles, and how these business processes are controlled.

COBIT® originally adapted its definition of control from COSO in that the policies, procedures, practices, and organizational structures are designed to provide reasonable assurance that business objectives will be achieved and that undesired events will be prevented or detected and corrected. COBIT® emphasizes the role and impact of IT control as they relate to business processes, whereas COSO defined internal control, described its components, and provided criteria against which control systems could be evaluated. In order for IT to facilitate effectiveness, a clear understanding of the organizational value chain is required in order to optimize the business processes in that chain. Porter[*] identified five activities within a typical value chain, namely:

- Inbound logistics
- Operations
- Outbound logistics
- Marketing and sales
- Service

At each stage of the value chain, IT can enable the organization to differentiate the value provided to its clients from its competition. IT can assist in driving down costs in order to create a low-cost differentiation or can be used to reconfigure the value chain to create a value-added differentiation.

Technology has become a critical component to business processes. IS Auditing responsibilities include the development and implementation of a risk-based IS Audit strategy and objectives in compliance with generally accepted audit standards (GAAS) in order to provide a statement of assurance that the organization's information technology and business processes are controlled, monitored, and assessed adequately, and are aligned with the organization's business objectives.

Such understandings of both the business process and the IT environment imply a collaborative approach because the IS auditor is rarely as knowledgeable about the process as the manager who routinely controls it or the IT staff implementing the IT control environment. By the same token, the management and IT teams who are involved in a business or IT process on a day-to-day basis will normally lack the independent perspective an internal auditor can bring to risk evaluation.

IT systems supporting such business processes may take several forms. The most basic types of systems are those that are used on an ongoing basis to provide facilities for the day-to-day operations of the organization. These normally involve the processing of everyday business transactions. Transaction processing systems include:

- Order processing
- Inventory
- Purchasing

---

[*] M. E. Porter, 'What is Strategy?' *Harvard Business Review*, vol. 74, no. 6, 1996.

In addition to these systems supporting normal business processing, management requires information on an ongoing basis to inform them of the status of various parts of the organization. These Management Information Systems would include:

- Financial
- Manufacturing
- Marketing
- Personnel

A further categorization of systems comes when the information becomes used by a variety of decision makers to support business decisions. These Decision Support Systems are becoming more and more sophisticated and may be found in all business areas including:

- Financial
- Statistical analysis
- Project management

IT projects are typically intended to deliver business value by automating business processes. Where business projects are enabled by technology, IT may be seen to be adding value to the organization. In general, automating business processes typically results in higher IT costs and lower business costs (or higher revenue).

The auditor may also have to take into consideration the Capability Maturity Model (CMM) which is a technique for evaluating and measuring process maturity within the organization. Business Processes may be classified as:

- **Level 5 – Optimized.** This is the highest rating level where business processes have the objectives for improvement defined and continuously revised in the light of changing business needs and objectives.
- **Level 4 – Managed.** At this level business processes are quantifiable and predictable at a detailed level with precise control criteria.
- **Level 3 – Defined.** Processes at this level are clearly documented and well understood, and have clearly defined objectives, standards, with quantitative measuring criteria.

- **Level 2 – Repeatable.** Using the appropriate management techniques, process is controlled using documented procedures and process definitions.
- **Level 1 – Initial.** Organizations operating at this level do not typically have a stable business environment with business processes being unique and outputs dependent on specific individuals.

The higher the business maturity level, in general, the greater the effectiveness to be expected from internal controls. This is particularly true when control structures have been designed in line with internationally accepted control models.

Control Principles Related to Controls in Information Systems

Overall, internal control objectives, at a detailed level, can be seen to encompass:

Reliability and Integrity of Information

If management cannot trust the reliability and integrity of the information held and processed within the IT, then all information must be deemed suspect and, in some cases, this may be more detrimental to the organization than a loss of information systems.

Compliance with Policies, Plans, Procedures, Laws, and Regulations

Laws and regulations are imposed externally and must be complied with. Inadequate information systems may lead to the organization inadvertently breaching the laws of the country resulting in losses in terms of fines, penalties, and possibly imprisonment for corporate officers.

The organization's internal policies, plans, and procedures are designed to ensure planned, systematic, and orderly operation. From time to time the manager may be required to evaluate the adequacy of such policies, plans, and procedures since the nature of the business may have changed, risks may have to be reassessed and control objectives re-prioritized.

Safeguarding of Assets

Loss of assets is typically one of the most visible risks an organization can face and typically these lead to the implementation of the most visible controls, such as locks on doors, safes, security guards, and so forth. In an IT-dependent organization, asset controls may also include non-tangibles such as dual custody, segregation of duties, and computer authentication techniques. Few organizations would be in a position to declare the information held as a corporate asset on the balance sheet. Nevertheless, the corporate information warehouse may be the largest asset the organization can claim if leveraged appropriately. In addition, for many organizations the financial records held within the computer systems are indeed actual assets in that, for example, the total value of inventory is commonly taken to be whatever the computer system says the inventory value is.

Similarly, debtor and creditor valuations are largely based upon the information contained within the appropriate computer systems.

Effectiveness and Efficiency of Operations

Effectiveness involves the achievement of established objectives and should be the ultimate focus of all operations and controls. Many information systems, at the time of the original design, were focused upon achieving the corporate objectives. Over time these objectives may have changed, and the information systems may become counterproductive to achieving those objectives. Computer systems therefore require constant monitoring as to their alignment with corporate strategic directions and intent.

In order for IT to facilitate effectiveness, a clear understanding of the organizational value chain is required in order to optimize the business processes in that chain. Porter[*] identified five activities within a typical value chain, namely:

- Inbound logistics
- Operations
- Outbound logistics
- Marketing and sales
- Service

---

[*] M. E. Porter, 'What is Strategy?' Harvard Business Review, vol. 74, no. 6, 1996.

Efficiency is classed as a measurement of the optimization of utilization of 'scarce resources' and includes reduction of waste as well as the reduction in underutilization of resources. In many organizations information systems have become the proverbial 'sledgehammer to crack a nut' and, taking only the case of office automation, have served to reduce efficiencies instead of improving them.

With those control objectives in mind, management can structure the system of internal controls to improve the probability of achieving all of those objectives.

In order to ensure that control over the corporate computer investment is adequate, a range of controls is required, including:

- **General IT controls.** Covering the environment within which the computer systems are utilized.
- **Computer operations.** Covering the day-to-day operations of the machine.
- **Physical security.** Covering the security of the physical hardware, software, buildings, and staff.
- **Logical security.** Covering the manner in which data and software are protected from access via the systems themselves.
- **Program change control.** To ensure that systems that are correct and functional and continue to be so.
- **Systems development.** To ensure that the systems in use by the organization are effective, efficient, and economical.

Risk-Based Audit Planning and Audit Project Management Techniques

Good corporate governance today dictates that businesses should understand their major risks and put in place appropriate controls to manage them effectively, so the business is more likely to achieve its objectives.

Those planning IS Auditing department activities face the recurrent task of allocating expected resources to an apparently ever-expanding universe of demands. One means of focusing limited resources is the use of appropriate risk analysis techniques. There are three types of risk that are normally considered when using a risk-based audit approach. They are *inherent risk*, *control risk*, and *detection risk*, which is also known as audit risk.

Inherent Risk

Inherent risk is the *likelihood of a significant loss occurring before taking into account any risk-reducing factors.* In evaluating inherent risk, an auditor must consider what the types and nature of risks are, as well as what factors indicate that a risk exists. To achieve this, he/she must be familiar with the environment in which the entity operates.

Control Risk

Control risk measures the likelihood that the control processes established to limit or manage inherent risk are ineffective. In order to ensure that an internal audit evaluates the controls properly, an auditor must understand how to measure which controls are effective. This will involve identifying those controls that provide the most assurance that risks are being minimized within the business. Control effectiveness is strongly affected by the quality of work and control supervision.

Controls in business operations provide the major defense against inherent risk. In general, an auditor may assume that stronger controls reduce the amount of risk; however, at some point, the cost of control may become prohibitive (in terms of both financial and staff resources, as well as customer satisfaction).

Audit Risk

Audit risk is *the risk that audit coverage will not address significant business exposures.* Pro forma audit programs can be developed in order to reduce audit risk. These provide guidance as to which key controls should exist to address the risk, and the recommended compliance and/or substantive test steps that should be performed. These programs should be used with care and modified to reflect the current business risk profile.

Planning the Audit Project

In planning the audit, auditors must define the audit objectives as well as the scope and methodology to achieve those objectives. Audit objectives, scope, and methodologies are not determined in isolation.

Auditors determine these three elements of the audit plan together, as the considerations in determining each often overlap. Planning is a continuous process throughout the audit. Therefore, auditors should consider the need to make adjustments to the audit objectives, scope, and methodology as the work is being completed.

Risk analysis includes:

- Estimating the significance of the risk
- Assessing the likelihood or frequency of the risk
- Considering how the risk should be managed
  - What actions need to be taken
  - What controls need to be effected
    - Preventative procedures – reduce the significance or likelihood of the risk occurring
    - Displacement procedures – offset the effect if it does occur
- Risks are normally evaluated before the mitigating effects of controls are considered
- Estimating the velocity, including the assessing by the organization of:
  - Speed of onset

  - How quickly does the risk descend upon us?
  - Do we have much warning?

  - Speed of impact

  - Do we feel the effects right away, or does the pain slowly increase?
  - Does it spread and impact us in other ways, e.g. reputation?

  - Speed of reaction

  - Even if we see it coming, do we have the agility to react in a timely way?

Risk factors may include factors such as the date and results of the last audit as well as the financial exposure and potential loss and risk. Major changes in operations, programs, systems, and controls as well as opportunities to achieve operating benefits can have a dramatic impact on operational risk.

Quality of the Internal Control Framework

The overall corporate control environment includes the governance and management functions, and the attitudes, awareness, and actions of those responsible for the governance and management of an organization's internal controls. The control environment sets the tone of an organization, influencing the control consciousness of its people, and is the foundation for effective control, providing discipline and structure. The control environment will include the following elements:

- Communication and enforcement of integrity and ethical values
- Commitment to competence and service
- Independent review and monitoring functions
- Management's philosophy and operating style, including its approach to taking and managing business risks
- Organizational structure and the framework for achieving the organization's business objectives
- Assignment of authority and responsibility
- Human resource policies and practices

As far as the specific control procedures themselves are concerned, the elements making up an effective internal control framework include:

- A good audit trail whereby transactions can be traced to their recording in the accounting information system and the recorded information can be traced back to the originating transaction documentation
- Safeguarding of assets to minimize the risks of damage to assets as well as theft
- Management reviews of control procedures to ensure, on an ongoing basis, their ability to mitigate risk to an acceptable level
- Competent and ethical employees to ensure that the individuals responsible for implementing internal control are both capable and honest
- Segregation of inappropriate organizational responsibilities to ensure asset custody, transaction authorization, and reconciliations are performed by separate individuals

Competence of Management

Underpinning the control system are the people who enforce it. In order for controls to be effective, those who exercise control must be capable of doing so (*competence*) and honest enough to consistently do so (*integrity*).

Complexity of Transactions

Today's business processes transmit more information across the network and increase the number and complexity of transactions. The more complex the transaction, the greater the chance that errors will proliferate and remain undetected.

Liquidity of Assets

Liquidity is the term commonly used to describe how easy it is to convert assets to cash. Obviously, the most liquid asset is cash itself, but in today's IT-dominated business environment, the records and data, together with the Intellectual Property held within IT systems may make the need to convert assets to cash redundant.

Ethical Climate and Employee Morale

Ethical climate refers to the way an organization conducts its business: how it treats people customers, staff, and suppliers, interacts with communities, and impacts the environment. Essentially, it is about corporate and individual actions and decisions. There is no single set of principles that define ethical behavior.

Ethical theories have evolved over the centuries, but it is useful to understand that the general areas of economic activity where management makes decisions often present tensions between ethical and legal choices. Rossouw[*] identifies three main areas:

- The macro- or systemic dimension, consisting of the policy framework created by the state, which determines the basis for economic exchanges both nationally and internationally

---

[*] Rossouw, D. 2002. Business Ethics in Africa. 2nd ed. Cape Town: Oxford University Press Southern Africa.

- The meso- or institutional dimension, consisting of the relations among economic organizations, such as public sector entities, private sector entities, private individuals, and those outside the organizations
- The micro- or intra-organizational dimension, consisting of the economic actions and decisions of individuals within an organization

Business executives are faced with the challenges of making ethical decisions in complex competitive business environments with multiple goals and objectives on a daily basis. Given the dynamic and constantly changing regulatory environment in which business operates on a global basis, decisions made by management could affect both the ethical image of the organization as well as employee morale.

Auditor Understanding of the Applicable Laws and Regulations That Affect the Scope, Evidence Collection and Preservation, and Frequency of Audits

Unlike policies, plans, and procedures, which are internally dictated by the organization, laws, and regulations are imposed externally and must be complied with. Inadequate information systems may lead to the organization inadvertently breaching the laws of the country resulting in losses in terms of fines, penalties, and possibly even imprisonment for corporate officers.

A corporate security policy must therefore spell out in detail that in protecting its information assets, the organization will comply with all applicable laws and regulations and will ensure that its employees will do so also. Auditing compliance, under these circumstances, means that IT auditors must have an in-depth understanding of the applicable laws and regulations that affect the scope, evidence collection and preservation, and frequency of audits

The audit schedule should therefore be linked, not only to current business objectives and risks based on their relative cost, but also in terms of the risks inherent in non-compliance with laws and regulations.

There are a plethora of international laws and regulations, fortunately, there are also tools that can help an organization identify laws and regulations and track the control processes implemented to address them.[*]

Evidence Collection Techniques

Auditors are commonly required to express an opinion on the adequacy and effectiveness of internal controls. For this, audit evidence must be gathered to support the opinion. Evidence is something intended to prove or support a belief. Each individual piece may be flawed by a personal bias or by a potential error of measurement, and each piece may be less competent than desirable, so the auditor must look at the total 'body of evidence', which should provide a factual basis for audit opinions.

For Internal Auditors, IIA Practice Advisory 2310-1: Identifying Information provides guidance as to the quality of the evidence that an internal auditor looks for.

> Information should be sufficient, competent, relevant, and useful to provide a sound basis for engagement observations and recommendations. Sufficient information is factual, adequate, and convincing so that a prudent, informed person would reach the same conclusions as the auditor. Competent information is reliable and the best attainable through the use of appropriate engagement techniques. Relevant information supports engagement observations and recommendations and is consistent with the objectives for the engagement. Useful information helps the organization meet its goal.[†]

The IS auditor usually obtains audit evidence by:

- Observing conditions
- Interviewing people
- Examining records

This is done in a variety of ways and generally follows the Audit Program. The Audit Program itself is a set of detailed steps that the auditor will follow in order to gain the appropriate evidence and, for the IS Auditor, may well include the use of computerized techniques,

---

[*] Filipek, R., Compliance automation, Internal Auditor, February 2007, pp. 27–29
[†] IIA Practice Advisory 2310-1

although this is not always the case. The actual program used will vary from audit to audit depending on what the auditor wishes to find out and must always include a degree of flexibility to allow for changes based on the evidence gathered.

For example, the auditor may wish to examine data files in order to determine that the printouts relied upon by management match the live data files. In such a case, the use of computer-assisted tools and techniques would be appropriate. In a different scenario, an auditor wishing to examine the authorization of transactions may use such tools to do extractions of records in order to do a follow-up on the documentary evidence of original documents seeking authorized signatures.

Again, for Internal Auditors, IIA Practice Advisory 2240-1:[*] Engagement Work Program gives the procedures that an internal auditor uses to gather audit evidence.

> Engagement procedures, including the testing and sampling techniques employed, should be selected in advance, where practicable, and expanded or altered if circumstances warrant.

There are various types of audit evidence:

- Physical evidence is generally obtained by observing people, property, or events and may take the form of photographs, maps, etc. Where the evidence is from observation, it should be supported by documented examples or, if not possible, by corroborating observation.
- Testimonial evidence may take the form of letters, statements in response to inquiries, or interviews and is not conclusive since these documents are only someone's opinion. It should be supported by documentation where possible.
- Documentary evidence is the usual form of audit evidence and includes letters, agreements, contracts, directives, memoranda, and other business documents. The source of the document will affect its reliability and the trust we place in it. The quality of internal control procedures will also be taken into account.

---

[*] IIA Practice Advisory 2240-1

- Analytical evidence is usually derived from computations, comparisons to standards, past operations, and similar operations. Regulations and common reasoning will also produce evidence of this kind.

Much of the evidence gathered by IS auditors fall into Documentary and Analytical classes.

Audit Techniques

The auditor will use test transaction techniques to review system level activity. In advanced auditing, the use of knowledge-based systems will permit the distribution of advanced audit techniques to less skilled staff.

Transaction test techniques could include:

Test data – This technique involves the utilization of a copy of the live computer system through which a series of transactions is passed in order to produce predetermined results. This technique, while effective in searching for defects, is limited by the volume of data that can be handled. In addition, the results may be biased by the results the auditor expects.

Integrated Test Facility (ITF) – This technique, while similar in nature to test data, is effected by creation within the live system, of a dummy entity (department, warehouse etc.) and the processing of test data against the dummy entity together with the live data. This technique has the advantages of testing the system as it normally operates, and testing both the computer and manual systems. It has distinct disadvantages as well. All test transactions must be removed from the live system before they affect live totals, postings, or the production of negotiable documents such as checks. In addition, there may be a very real danger of destroying the live system. ITFs must be used with great care.

Source-code review – This computer audit technique involves the review of the source code originally written by the programmer. In the past this has meant browsing through piles of printout. In today's environment, sophisticated searches can be implemented using generalized audit software to establish weaknesses in the source code.

Embedded audit modules (SCARFs - System Collection Audit Review Files) – In systems where audit trails may only exist as computer records and then only for a short time or discontinuously, it may be necessary for the auditor to have in-built a facility to collect and retain selected information to serve as an audit trail for subsequent examination. This obviously makes the collected data a target for destruction or manipulation and it must be treated as such.

Parallel Simulation – Parallel simulation is a technique involving the creation of software to simulate some functional capability of the live system such as a calculation. The live data is processed through the simulating program in parallel with the live system and the outputs are compared.

Review of system level activity involves the examination of control areas with a pervasive influence such as telecoms, the operating environment itself, the systems development function, and change control.

End-User Computing, although not in the same category of general control can be treated in the same manner as a general threat.

Automated Audit Tools

The Computer Assisted Audit Tools (CAATs) used will include Test Data Generators for testing all or selected parts of application systems. Flowcharting Packages to document data flows and controls. Certainty of the more sophisticated systems may require the use of Specialized Audit Software to carry out tasks that are unique to the audit of that type of system and which, due to the nature of the systems and file structures, etc., could not effectively be carried out by Generalized Audit Software.

Generalized Audit Software (GAS) is standard software produced for auditors to permit nonprogrammers to carry out a variety of normal audit procedures on a variety of systems. They are designed to be as flexible as possible while remaining as user-friendly as possible. Utility programs are those standard software products that handle everyday facilities such as sort, copy, print, backup, restore etc. They can be invaluable audit tools in a complicated systems environment.

Non audit-specific software includes those programs which were never designed as audit tools but may easily be utilized by auditors. They include report writers and general interrogation packages.

In addition to these tools, the auditor has available automated tools to assist in the areas of risk analysis and audit planning. Automated working papers are possible using certain software packages and, in an extensive audit of a complicated and integrated system, such a tool may be invaluable.

Automated tools (CAATs) will commonly be used and these may include:

- *Test Data Generators* – Automatic producers of data for systems testing. These take away the drudgery of preparing test data to try out the various pathways through systems as well as ensuring that all desired avenues of testing are carried out.
- *Flowcharting Package* – This audit tool is becoming increasingly popular with auditors who wish to document information flow, control points, and operational procedures. Such packages allow the maintaining of up-to-date records with a minimum of re-work.
- *Specialized Audit Software* – Specialized audit software is software written explicitly to achieve some desired audit objective. It may be utilized for any purpose the auditor chooses but, because it was designed to achieve specific ends, it may prove inflexible where audit objectives and sources of evidence are rapidly changing. In addition, such software is typically expensive to develop since there is a limited market.
- *Generalized Audit Software* – This is some of the most common software in use by auditors today. It incorporates general interrogation routines as well as statistical sampling and pre-fabricated audit tests. This is seen to be the major growth area for CAATs over the next few years particularly in its use for data analytics.
- *Utility Programs* – This software, supplied with the hardware or systems software, is designed to perform common and repetitive tasks such as sorting files, printing, copying, and comparing files.

As such these can be powerful tools for the auditor to employ. Because of the power of some of these utilities, special authorities may be required to access the requested data. Determining which of these tools would be appropriate to a large extent depends on the audit objective and selected technique. These techniques are normally performed for one of two objectives. Either to verify processing operations or to verify the results of processing. No single technique is infallible. and none tells the whole story so that the auditor will typically choose a variety of techniques in order to satisfy multiple objectives.

Domain 1 – Examination Tips

It is not uncommon for highly skilled IS auditors to fail to pass the CISA on the first attempt. It is not a lack of knowledge but the wrong approach to the examination as a whole, and the questions in particular, which cause these problems. These tips form a guide to assist candidates for the CISA examination to avoid some of the pitfalls.

Questions within the CISA examination fall into two broad categories, namely:

- Conceptual questions which test the auditor's understanding of both auditing standards and fundamental risks and control opportunities within information systems
- Practical questions requiring an auditor to interpret a scenario and apply both the appropriate standards as well as understanding the risks inherent in the scenario, the appropriateness of controls selected, the types of tests which would be appropriate, and the nature recommendations to mitigate any weaknesses found

In many of the examination questions, the candidate may be given a scenario of potential risk areas and be asked to make a choice in terms of business risk. Alternatively, the auditor may be given the scenario together with the controls implemented and be asked to identify either the best or the least effective control. It is critical that the candidate clearly understands the questions and answers the question *asked* and not the question candidate believes *should have been asked* or the examiner *meant to ask*.

In many of these scenarios the experienced IS auditor may find that, based on their own personal experience, none of the answers is *fully* correct all, alternatively, all of the answers *could* be correct. The candidate must always remember that the questions are being asked based on what is *supposed* to happen in the best case scenario and in line with the appropriate standards and not what happened the last time the candidate encountered such a situation in real life. Such questions are testing the candidate's judgment in terms of best practice.

CISA tests best practice in general. Technical questions on generic technology such as Internet Security, control over telecommunications, encryption, Electronic Data Interchange will occur occasionally but technology-specific platform questions such specific technology brands, SQL, IDMS, Z/OS, and the like are not normally questioned and candidates are not expected to study every technology component available.

Not all questions are created equal and the danger is that the candidate, having answered what would appear to be obvious questions, will assume that all questions will have clear meanings and therefore obvious answers. CISA questions are frequently written to test the candidate's ability to think logically through the question to derive the most appropriate answer. In all cases questions should be read quickly, *but carefully*, and analyzed word by word to derive the actual question being asked. Where the answer appears to be purely subjective based upon an auditor's opinion, reread the questions to ensure the underlying meaning is fully understood before an answer is selected. Remember, you are looking for the correct ISACA answer and not necessarily what your own experience dictates.

When the candidate encounters a question where all of the answers appear correct or none of the answers appear correct, candidates should be aware that many of such questions will have at least one choice as an obviously wrong answer. Be careful that such distracting answers are not, in fact, the correct answer. Where the auditor is sure that the answer is genuinely incorrect, eliminate that choice and focus on the remaining answers seeking the one which *best* answers the question asked.

My recommendation is to ensure that no question remains unanswered. A common trap is to leave the question so that the auditor can come back to it. If you run out of time you may have no opportunity to go back. Answering incorrectly is better than not answering since the examination is positively marked, that is incorrect answers do not get more negatively marked and a best guess which may have a 50/50 chance of being correct is better than no guess and therefore no chance of a mark.

Domain 1 – Practice Questions

1. According to the Standards, internal auditors review information systems to:
   a. Become familiar with the activities and controls to be audited, to identify areas for audit emphasis, and to invite auditee comments.
   b. Ensure that application systems meet management's defined, authorized requirements and determine if they are likely to continue to do so.
   c. Determine that financial and operating records and reports contain accurate, reliable, timely, complete, and useful information.
   d. Ensure that systems under development incorporate adequate controls and that the implementation of the controls will be effective.

2. IS auditors are required to have skills in:
   a. Management processes.
   b. Technical processes within the organization.
   c. Understanding of IS risks and the use of appropriate control structures.
   d. Implementing IS controls.

3. Understanding the business process involves:
   a. Identifying and examining the key activities.
   b. Designing and implementing control structures.
   c. Defining performance objectives.
   d. Selecting control strategies.

4. For controls to be effective, they must be:
   a. Monitored continuously.

b. Designed by IS auditors.

c. Designed by internal auditors.

d. Audited on a daily basis.

5. IS Auditing professionalism is normally indicated by:

   a. Employing professional IS auditors.

   b. Outsourcing the IS audit function.

   c. Employing professional internal auditors.

   d. Compliance with internationally recognized standards.

6. Reasons for outsourcing IS audit could include:

   a. Lack of funds.

   b. Lack of in-house skills.

   c. Lack of time.

   d. Lack of direction.

7. IS auditors may use a tool called 'risk analysis' in preparing work schedules. Which of the following would not be considered in performing a risk analysis?

   a. Financial exposure and potential loss.

   b. Skills available on the audit staff.

   c. Results of prior audits.

   d. Major operating changes.

8. Factors that should be considered when evaluating audit risk in an IS functional area include:

   1. Volume of transactions.

   2. Degree of system integration.

   3. Years since last audit.

   4. Significant management turnover.

   5. Value of 'assets at risk'.

   6. Average value per transaction.

   7. Results of last audit.

   Factors that best define materiality of audit risk are:

   a. 1 through 7.

   b. 2, 4, and 7.

   c. 1, 5, and 6.

   d. 3, 4, and 6.

9. A risk which measures the likelihood that a control process is not effective is an example of:
   a. Inherent risk.
   b. Audit risk.
   c. Control risk.
   d. Failure risk.

10. The core of the information processing architecture is the:
    a. Organization's data.
    b. Mainframe communications.
    c. Mainframe computer.
    d. Servers.

11. Key controls to mitigate risk are tested in order to determine the risk is being controlled in a manner which is:
    a. Adequate and effective.
    b. Adequate.
    c. At the level specified by management.
    d. Effective.

12. A risk arising external to the organization which calls for a risk position to be taken by the organization is:
    a. An influenceable risk.
    b. A controllable risk.
    c. An uncontrollable risk.
    d. A strategic risk.

13. Risk mitigation can be achieved by any of the following except:
    a. Risk avoidance.
    b. Risk elimination.
    c. Risk transference.
    d. Risk assumption.

14. In gathering evidence an auditor will:
    a. Always use computer assisted audit tools and techniques.
    b. Use whichever tools and techniques are appropriate for the audit.
    c. Use the same audit program as last year.
    d. Design an audit program and follow it exactly.

15. ISACA standards:
    a. Are mandatory for all IS auditors.
    b. Give guidelines only and auditors may deviate where they feel appropriate.
    c. Give procedures only but do not set requirements.
    d. Are designed for the use of auditors only.

16. COSO standards regarding information systems address:
    a. Accuracy and completeness of data input.
    b. Internally generated data used by the organization.
    c. Timeliness of external information gathering.
    d. The effective flow of communications throughout the organization.

17. IS risks should be:
    a. Controlled at all costs.
    b. Eliminated completely.
    c. Accepted as a normal part of doing business.
    d. Subject to a management control process.

18. A commonly encountered problem as a result of computer risks is:
    a. Business interruption.
    b. Major changes to operations, programs, systems, and controls.
    c. Improvements in ethical climate and employee morale.
    d. Increased insurance costs.

19. Inherent risk can be defined as:
    a. The risk that significant business exposures have not been adequately addressed by the audit process.
    b. The likelihood of a significant loss occurring before taking into account the risk reducing factors.
    c. The risk which is left after control procedures have been implemented.
    d. The likelihood that the control processes established to manage risks have proved to be ineffective.

20. Computer risks, exposures, and losses are:
    a. Always unintentional.

   b. Always intentional.

   c. The result of failure within the control systems.

   d. Controllable only to a certain extent.

21. The most common source of IT threats is:
   a. Management.
   b. IS Auditors.
   c. Users.
   d. Outsiders.

22. The primary reason for an IS risk-based audit approach is:
   a. To control costs within the IS function.
   b. To permit the efficient allocation of limited IS audit resources.
   c. To show management the areas in which the controls are deficient.
   d. To show the audit committee that IS audit is being carried out in an appropriate manner.

23. The starting point for risk-based audit approach is:
   a. Determination of the overall business objectives of the organization.
   b. Determination of the individual detailed control objectives.
   c. Identification of the internal controls relied upon by management.
   d. Identification of best practice in selecting internal controls.

24. Discretionary audit activities of those activities which:
   a. Must be carried out within the timespan of the audit plan.
   b. Are based upon management's requests.
   c. Are decided upon using all risk factors.
   d. Are decided upon using only the most important risk factors.

25. Unknown internal controls indicate:
   a. A higher level of risk.
   b. A lower level of risk.
   c. An unacceptable level of risk.
   d. An acceptable level of risk.

Domain One – Review Questions and Hands-On Exercise

- Describe the need for IS auditing.
- Differentiate between the roles of Internal and External IS auditing.
- Describe the role of management and its relationship with audit.
- Define the role of the audit charter and describe its typical content.
- Describe the differences between the concepts of inherent risk, control risk, and audit risk.
- Differentiate among the types of IS risk.
- Differentiate among controllable, uncontrollable, and influenceable risks.
- Describe the different classifications of audit evidence.
- Describe the classifications of reliability of audit evidence.
- Define the audit role in fraud prevention and detection.
- Describe the nature of risk and its impact in a corporate environment.
- Explain the function of risk analysis and its applicability in IS auditing.
- Explain the use of risk-based auditing within an integrated approach.
- Explain the source of computer risks and their effects on the business.
- Describe common risk factors.
- Quantify the impacts of computer risks.
- Describe the elements and procedures of risk analysis.

Exercise 1. The IS auditors for Fast Fuse, a large electronics manufacturing company, are planning an audit of the central purchasing department. More specifically, the auditors intended to study the department's approved vendor listings in order to:

a) Determine whether the approved vendors were being used.
b) Evaluate the individual vendors approved for the listings in terms of availability of desired products, quality of products, prices, and timeliness of delivery.
c) Examine any potential conflicts of interest among corporate employees and approve vendors.

d) Evaluate how vendors are selected from the listings for individual orders when more than one approved vendor is listed.

The auditors have decided to interview the purchasing director, his assistant, and both purchasing clerks. They will also examine a statistical sample of purchase orders from the past three years and the first six months of this year. They plan to examine the approved listings and catalogs from the last four years for each of the approved vendors. Questionnaires will also be distributed among other departments of goods received through the purchasing department. The auditors plan to begin the audit on January 8th, 2018. Two auditors, Arthur Fourie and Mbazima Mwale, have been assigned to conduct the audit which is estimated to take seven days on site. The audit report will be distributed to Johnny Schoeman, the head of operations, Alfred Heath, director of central purchasing and the company audit committee.

Required:

Assuming the audit has already been prearranged by telephone with Mr. Heath, explain the risk factors involved for the upcoming audit and the methodology that will be used to carry out the audit.

Domain 1 – Answers to Practice Questions

1. **B** The primary objective of information system reviews is to ensure that management objectives are achieved. The other answers are all secondary objectives in conducting the review.

2. **C** Understanding of information systems risks is fundamental to the tasks of the IS auditor. Management and technical processes form part of the internal control structure to alleviate those risks and the implementation of controls is the method by which risk is mitigated.

3. **A** Control structures, performance objectives, and control strategies can only be formulated or audited after the business processes are fully understood.

4. **A** The ongoing continuous monitoring of controls is essential to ensure their effectiveness. Such controls should be designed by management and not by auditors.

5. **D** As with any profession, compliance with international standards is fundamental to displaying professionalism in the

execution of the function. Employing professional auditors is not a guarantee that the work will be carried out to professional standards and nor is outsourcing.

6. **B** Outsourcing of any function, due to the profit nature of an outsourcer, is generally more expensive and carrying out the function in-house subject to the availability of the appropriate skills. Management failure in directing the function or managing time will not be improved by simply outsourcing.

7. **B** Risk analysis would involve consideration of all operational risks as well as the results of prior audits. The availability or lack of skills within the audit function should not be considered since lack of skills may always be outsourced.

8. **A** All of those risk factors would form input to evaluate the risk in an IS functional area.

9. **C** Control risk occurs when the control process is not effective. Inherent risk is a risk given that no control exists, while audit risk is the risk of an auditor coming to the wrong conclusion, for example by conducting the wrong tests. Failure risk is simply the risk that an objective fails to be achieved.

10. **D** The information processing architecture is geared towards protection of the organization's data held upon the servers. The communications and computer itself are mechanisms by which control may be achieved.

11. **C** While adequacy and effectiveness of controls are desirable, the overall objective is to ensure the risk is controlled to the level specified by management.

12. **C** The definition of an uncontrollable risk is one outside the control of the organization where a risk position must be taken regarding the acceptability or not of the risk. The risk itself may not be controllable, but the impact of the risk may require management activity to mitigate.

13. **B** A variety of control techniques may be employed to avoid, or transfer risk or management may decide to accept or assume the risk. Generally, it must be held that while risks can be avoided, they cannot be eliminated.

14. **B** CAATs are only used where appropriate and may differ from the previous audit program if the audit objectives or

sources of evidence differ. The audit program itself should be looked on as provisional and may require to be varied as the audit proceeds depending upon the evidence uncovered.

15. **A** The ISACA standards are mandatory for all CISAs or ISACA members. In addition, they may be used by non-auditors.

16. **D** The COSO standards regarding information systems are intended to ensure an effective flow of communications. They do not directly dictate the accuracy and completeness of data or the timeliness of external data gathering.

17. **D** All information systems risks fall within the purview of management and are therefore subject to management control processes. Since the objective, as usual, is to reduce risk to a level acceptable to management in a cost-effective manner, control should not be sought 'at all costs'. Complete elimination of risk is not feasible while acceptance of risk is one of several alternatives.

18. **D** Business interruption may occur in the event of a risk occurrence transpiring while major changes may cause risk. Where risk occurs, ethical climate and morale may be negatively impacted, not improved

19. **B** Inherent risk is the risk of an untoward event occurring before taking into consideration the effect of risk-reducing factors. A) is a definition of audit risk, C) defines residual risk, and D) is the definition of control risk.

20. **D** Computer risks may sometimes be unintentional or even intentional. They may or may not occur as a result of failure within control systems, but they are always controllable only to a certain degree.

21. **C** Unfortunately, while all of the others are risk sources, the most common source remains users.

22. **B** Risk-based auditing may help with A), C), and D) but the intention is to allow audit resources to be focused on the areas of greatest risk and therefore permit the efficient allocation of such resources.

23. **A** The business objectives of the organization are the starting point for all control procedures and therefore the risks to the business objectives form the starting point of the risk-based

audit approach. All of the other alternatives will form part of the risk analysis itself.

24. **D** Mandatory audit activities are those which must be carried out within the timespan of the audit plan. Management requests, depending on their nature, maybe discretionary or mandatory. Discretionary activities are generally based upon the most significant risk factors.

25. **A** Where the extent or effectiveness of internal controls are unknown, the only safe assumption for the auditor is a higher level of risk.

Exercise 1 Sample Answer

The risk factors include:

- Poor quality of vendors
- Poor quality of vendor products
- Late deliveries
- Overpricing
- Employee conflict of interests
- Approval of inappropriate vendors
- Selection of wrong vendors
- The use of inappropriate vendors
- The unavailability of products from vendors
- Plus, other justifiable risk factors

Audit methodology to include:

- Direct interviews
- Analysis at a given confidence level from a selected population
- Examination of approval procedures
- Examinations selection procedures
- Examination of product price catalogs
- Use of questionnaires to departments receiving goods
- Direct contact with vendors
- Trend analysis of vender usage
- Analysis of sole supplier status
- Analysis of track record of vendors used in the past
- Plus, other justifiable techniques

3

DOMAIN 2 – GOVERNANCE AND MANAGEMENT OF IT

This chapter covers the processes involved in providing assurance that the necessary leadership and organizational structures and processes are in place to achieve objectives and to support the organization's strategy and the areas covered within the CISA examination. As has been noted, this domain approximates 16% of the examination, that is some 24 questions. Ten tasks and 17 knowledge statements are included within this domain.

Governance in General

The importance of good governance is widely recognized internationally and is driven by the requirements of the global economy for transparency, accountability, and a shareholder-inclusive approach to economic, social, and environmental stewardship.

Three significant governance frameworks have become widely recognized as IT governance frameworks, namely ITIL, ISO/IEC 38508, and COBIT®. Although each of these has significant strengths in the fields of IT governance, none provide a complete IT governance solution.

Within COBIT®, IT governance is closely aligned with international accepted principles of good corporate governance and is intrinsically acceptable to regulators as well as multiple layers of management. It also facilitates connectivity to the ITIL and ISO frameworks. For purposes of the CISA examination, COBIT® forms the primary structure used within the examination and is a balance between the *minimization of IT risks* and *the creation of corporate value*. COBIT® classifies the overall objectives of IT governments as:

- Ensuring strategic orientation, focusing on corporate solutions

- The creation of benefits, focusing on optimizing the tasks and assessing the benefit of the IT
- Implementation of Risk Management relating to the protection of the IT assets and taking account of disaster recovery and continuation of the corporate processes in the event of a crisis
- Effective Resource Management in order to ensure the optimization of knowledge and infrastructure
- Adequacy of Performance Measurement and the creation of the bases for continual improvement

Principle 5 of COBIT® involves the separation of governance from management and draws the distinction COBIT® 5 makes between governance and management. This distinction is closely aligned to the guidance in ISO/IEC 38500.* COBIT® 5 differentiates the processes encompassing different types of IT activities between governance and IT management. The governance processes are organized following the EDM (Evaluate, Direct, Monitor) model, laid out in ISO/IEC 38500. IT governance processes ensure that enterprise objectives are achieved by:

- Evaluating stakeholder needs
- Setting direction through prioritization and decision-making
- Monitoring performance, compliance, and progress against plans

IT governance is attributed to the accountability of the board of directors or equivalent. It is upon these governance activities that business and IT management plans, builds, runs, and monitors activities.

IT governance has been defined as 'specifying the framework for decision rights and accountabilities to encourage desirable behavior and the use of IT'.† Overall, it is seen to be less about the specific decisions made and more about determining which decisions are to be made, who makes each type of decision, how decisions are arrived at, and who will be held accountable for the results of the decision.

---

* International Organization for Standardization (ISO) and International Electrotechnical Commission (IEC), ISO/IEC 38500:2008, Corporate governance of information technology, 2008, http://www.iso.org

† Weill, Peter, and Ross, Jeanne W., 'IT Governance on One Page', 2004, MIT Center for InformationSystems Research (CISR) WP 349.2

As with any other form of governance, IT governance directs the IT operations to ensure alignment with the enterprise in order to realize the promised benefits by exploiting opportunities and maximizing benefits. IT governance is also specified as a requirement in both national and international legislation such as the Sarbanes Oxley Act, 2002, in the USA, and the Basel Accords governing financial institutions.

The role of the IT auditor is critical to the success of IT governance and the audit, control, and security of IT.

Ultimately, IT Governance is a management responsibility, and therefore not the sole responsibility of an audit function although Internal and IT Audit may be tools used by management in the process. The audit function is required to remain independent but may be in a unique position to influence and recommend change. Many auditors believe that to maintain their independence the provision of advice should be limited. Where such advice is given, the individual auditor may be compromised in subsequently auditing the appropriateness or adequacy of the internal control structures, but the audit function, as a whole, is not compromised. In addition, with management owning the accountability for implementation and operation of controls, auditing the effectiveness of the control structure as implemented will not be compromised, even for the recommending auditor. IT Governance is a function of the overall management commitment and ownership within IT. Audit is therefore in a position to evaluate whether it is happening, and its overall effectiveness. This goes beyond simply identifying the existence of problems. Auditors must identify root causes within control structures and make the appropriate corrective recommendations.

The increasing reliance on self-assessments by IT management is also changing the role of the audit function, with audit assisting management in identifying appropriate standards, and control criteria coupled with control benchmarks.

The first task designated for the IS auditor within this domain involves the evaluation of the integrated corporate IT strategy. This involves both the overall IT direction, as well as the processes within the organization designed and implemented to ensure the strategy's development, approval, implementation, and maintenance for alignment with the organization's strategies and objectives.

With this as a basis, the auditor would seek to determine whether IT decisions, directions and performance are in line with and support the organization's strategies and objectives in order to determine the effectiveness of the general IT governance structure.

One of the critical elements in conducting an evaluation would be to determine whether the overall IT structure and human resources management processes are aligned to the organizational strategies and objectives. Coupled with this, the corporate IT policies, standards, and procedures would be examined to ensure the support for both the IT strategy and the regulatory and legal requirements for the organization. In addition to examining the overall policies, standards, and procedures, the auditor would evaluate the processes for their development, approval, implementation, and maintenance.

A critical component of IT governance involves the management processes governing the investment, prioritization, allocation, and use of IT resources and portfolio management ensuring their alignment, once again, with the corporate strategies and objectives.

The overall IT governance requires the implementation of the appropriate risk management practices covering the identification, assessment, monitoring, reporting, and managing of IT risk. With the risk appetite known and evaluated, the monitoring of controls to mitigate risk such as quality assurance in IT activities can be audited against predetermined managerial targets. These targets are based on IT's identification of their key performance areas (KPAs) and key performance indicators (KPIs) which ensure management acquires sufficient information on critical measurement criteria to ensure an adequate and timely response to any deficiencies noted.

Where the auditor determines that all policies, procedures, and monitoring mechanisms are in place and effective, the focus moves to ensuring the organization's ability to maintain critical business operations and procedures during any periods of IT disruption arising from whichever source, internal or external, through the use of an effective business continuity plan (BCP).

ISACA has defined specific knowledge statements required of the IT auditor and which may be examined, including:

- Knowledge of the purpose of IT strategy, policies, standards, and procedures for an organization and the essential elements of each
- Knowledge of IT governance, management, security, and control frameworks, and related standards, guidelines, and practices

- Knowledge of the organizational structure, roles and responsibilities related to IT, including segregation of duties (SoD)
- Knowledge of the relevant laws, regulations, and industry standards affecting the organization
- Knowledge of the organization's technology direction and IT architecture and their implications for setting long-term strategic directions
- Knowledge of the processes for the development, implementation, and maintenance of IT strategy, policies, standards and procedures
- Knowledge of the use of capability and maturity models
- Knowledge of process optimization techniques
- Knowledge of IT resource investment and allocation practices, including prioritization criteria (e.g. portfolio management, value management, personnel management)
- Knowledge of IT supplier selection, contract management, relationship management, and performance monitoring processes, including third-party outsourcing relationships
- Knowledge of enterprise risk management (ERM)
- Knowledge of the practices for monitoring and reporting of controls performance (e.g. continuous monitoring, quality assurance [QA])
- Knowledge of quality management and quality assurance (QA) systems
- Knowledge of the practices for monitoring and reporting of IT performance (e.g. balanced scorecard [BSC], key performance indicators [KPIs])
- Knowledge of business impact analysis (BIA)
- Knowledge of the standards and procedures for the development, maintenance, and testing of the business continuity plan (BCP)
- Knowledge of the procedures used to invoke and execute the business continuity plan (BCP) and return to normal operation[*]

IT Architecture

The overall IT architecture describes a series of principles, guidelines, and rules used by an enterprise to direct the overall process of

---

[*] http://www.isaca.org/Certification/CISA-Certified-Information-Systems-Auditor /Job-Practice-Areas/Pages/CISA-Job-Practice-Areas.aspx

acquiring, building, modifying, and interfacing IT resources across the enterprise.

IT Policies and Standards

The IT audit role in evaluating overall Policies and Standards lays out the tasks involved for the auditor in:

- IT processes
- Strategic planning
- The role of the IT steering committee
- Effective communication
- Organizational planning
- Portfolio management
- Demand management
- Project initiation
- Technical review
- Architecture and standards
- Enterprise and Business architectures
- Application, Information, and Infrastructure architectures

This includes Risk Management from the IT auditor's perspective and examines the processes involved in IT risk identification.

Common risks an organization may face from failures of IT security include:

- Loss of reputation
- Loss of confidentiality
- Loss of information integrity
- User authentication failure
- System unavailability

These risks, considered at a detailed level and rated based on the organizational criticality of the assets, are risks that can be used to identify the appropriate control mechanisms to secure communications and networks.

The overall risk will largely depend on entity objectives, and the identification must be seen as an iterative process carried out on an ongoing basis. During the risk assessment, IS auditors develop an understanding of the operation's business in order to facilitate the identification and assessment of significant risks to and from the information systems.

A sound risk assessment process requires the implementation of an awareness of the risks and obstacles to the successful achievement of business objectives and the development of an ability to deal with them. As such management must establish a set of objectives that integrate all the organization's resources so that the organization operates in unison. The risk assessment itself involves the identification, analysis, and management of the risks and obstacles to the successful achievement of the three primary business objectives, namely:

- Economy and efficiency of operations, including achievement of performance goals and safeguarding of assets against loss
- Reliable financial and operational data and reports
- Compliance with laws and regulations

Process and Quality Management includes the types of organizational structure appropriate within a given organization's IT function as well as the appropriate roles and responsibilities.

ISO Quality Management and Quality Assurance System Standards are incorporated in COBIT® 5 which forms the basis for CISA quality examination and includes the Capability Maturity Model Integration (CMMI). Critical IT processes require a *process framework* against which all critical processes may be defined, reviewed, validated, and maintained, while the overall policies and procedures of management dictate how the organization will be divided to efficiently control small portions of the company.

The need for effective financial management has become critical since IT now consumes a sizable proportion of the organization's budget. Different organizations utilized different pricing models to cost out IT services depending on the overall IT strategy and this can lead the auditor into corporate political disputes as such costing will impact the apparent efficiency of individual departments, be they corporate or governmental. Regardless of the pricing model chosen, the accurate tracking of IT utilization as well as the management of IT assets, both hardware and software, is essential and is an area for audit evaluation.

With CISA's structure aligning so closely with the COBIT® guidelines, project management processes may be seen to be essential in supporting an effective IT organization. The roles and controls surrounding IT Project Management are broken down by ISACA into:

- A project management life cycle (PMLC) that can be applied generically
- A development life cycle which addresses the specific needs of the application or other deliverable under consideration

The Project Management Institute (PMI) has published the Project Management Body of Knowledge (PMBOK)* which is taken to be the definitive work on the subject.

A project management framework or a PMLC (Project Management Life Cycle) is focused on the project scope, schedule, and budget, whereas the Systems Development Life Cycle or SDLC is focused on the analysis, construction, and testing.

Project management is intended to ensure the adequate definition of all project tasks, appropriate use of the resources available, efficient use of resources, and that quality is maintained to enable the project to be completed on time and within budget.

Project Management

Control Objectives for Information and Related Technology (COBIT®) defines control over the IT process as involving the need to 'determine the technology direction to support the business'.

Within this overall framework, a *project* may be defined as a temporary endeavor undertaken to accomplish a unique purpose, typically involving several people performing interrelated activities. In IS terms this would normally involve the bringing together of a variety of user and IS skills to work together in order to develop new or improved information systems. IT projects cover the specification, supply, and installation of 'off-the-shelf' systems as well as the development of bespoke software (i.e. software uniquely developed for a specific purpose). As with any other project-based development process, the primary focus of the project is the development of a quality system, as specified by the user, on time and within budget.

---

* https://www.pmi.org/pmbok-guide-standards/foundational/pmbok/sixth-edition

Each individual project will be unique in nature, although following a common plan or framework in as much as the system being developed will be unique and the individual combination of resources put together to achieve it will be unique. The project may be seen as a *finite, pre-defined* set of activities to lead to a *specific outcome*. It is finite in that it has a fixed beginning and a fixed end. It is predefined in that each individual phase of the project can be planned in advance and allowances made for changes during the development process. It is a set of individual activities that can be individually controlled but which must be coordinated in order to ensure that all areas fit together appropriately so that the project may achieve its specific outcomes.

Role of the Project Management Office (PMO)

In its role as the owner of the project management and program management process, the PMO is typically a permanent structure with staffing to provide professional support in maintaining current procedures and standards as well as developing new procedures and standards as opportunities for improvement of project and program management occur.

The IS auditor should be able to differentiate between auditing the application under development or review as opposed to the auditing of the project process itself.

In terms of the Project Portfolio within the PMO, *Portfolio Management* itself is intended to ensure the optimization of the project portfolio results as opposed to individual products or projects. This includes the scheduling and prioritization of individual projects including the coordination of both internal and external resources.

Ensuring the effectiveness of project portfolio management, an essential tool is a *project portfolio database*. A database will include individual project details of:

- Project type
- Project owner
- Schedules
- Project objectives
- Project status and costs

as well as reports covering the project portfolio itself.

In order to ensure that both IT and the business achieve their value management objectives, the PMO also monitors the *Project Benefits Realization* to ensure projects are delivered:

- As specified in a manner enabling measurable business value
- On time
- Within budget

Constant monitoring of project progress is essential to ensure management achieves the benefits intended. This would typically include:

- Definition of the intended benefits management wishes to derive
- Planning for the achievement of the benefit
- Deciding measurement and target criteria
- Assignment of realization responsibilities
- Ultimate evaluation of the delivered benefits

Computer projects, either involving the development or acquisition of new systems or the maintenance of existing systems, consume resources in terms of money, manpower, materials, machines, and methods. Many of these resources will be drawn from cross-departmental boundaries and will involve a mixture of skills and disciplines.

Resource Management

Information Resource Management is based on five fundamental principles:

1. **Information Management.** Information is valuable and needs to be managed as such. In many organizations, information, as such, does not appear on the balance sheet or asset register and is thus seen as something that, while important, is not really valuable.
2. **Technology Management.** Technology Management addresses the whole aspect of utilizing the value of technology to the firm. This includes the impact and effect

on other corporate resources as well as the gaining of strategic advantage by judicious use of the appropriate technology.

3. **Distributed Management.** Where systems are located, both physically and logically, can have a significant impact on systems effectiveness as well as internal control and thought must be given to the maintaining of an adequate system of managerial control.

4. **Functional Management.** Like other functional corporate areas, IT must be directed and controlled in order to ensure the effective, efficient, and economic use of what is, after all, a not inexpensive resource.

5. **Strategic Management.** IS holds the potential to gain and maintain a major competitive advantage for the organization. Used appropriately, IT can raise the barriers of entry to competition allowing effective domination of a market niche, gain exclusivity for the information holder, and generally keep the organization ahead of the pack.

Project management controls to assist the process involve periodic schedule reviews, work assignment, performance monitoring, progress monitoring, and status reporting and follow-up. In other words, an IT project is managed no differently than any other long-term, high-cost engineering project.

Project Planning

Confucius is quoted in *The Doctrine of the Mean* as stating: 'In all things, success depends upon previous preparation – and without such preparation there is sure to be failure'. This is the basis for all project planning. Project planning therefore involves working with user groups in order to ensure end-product alignment with business strategic planning. Within this constraint, project planning elements would include appropriate project guidelines, work breakdowns complete with start and completion dates, and an effective monitoring mechanism to measure against agreed schedules thus granting management appropriate project tracking and oversight capability. The project manager should therefore determine:

- The overall scope of the project in conjunction with project stakeholders
- A breakdown of the task elements required to deliver the expected system
- The order in which those task elements must be achieved
- The resources required, both IT and non-IT, to deliver each element
- The time required to deliver each element
- Budgeting and cost of each task

Determining the cost of developing or acquiring systems may take a variety of forms. A common technique, based on the experience of the project manager, is the use of estimates derived from private projects. This technique is known as *analogous estimating* and is popular because of its speed of use.

An *actual cost* technique would take an extrapolation from costs incurred on similar projects and similar systems.

Analogous estimating may be expanded on by using statistical data such as estimated material costs, technology in use, as well as knowledge of the skill availability within the employees assigned to the project. This technique is known as *parametric estimating*.

In the case of new or unique projects, a more laborious, and therefore more expensive, technique may be utilized. *Bottom-up estimating* involves estimating the duration and cost of each activity and then summing them to determine the cost estimate of the entire project. Although time consuming, this is typically the most accurate method of estimating both the cost and the duration of a project.

Function Point Analysis

Project complexity in large business applications may be evaluated using a technique called *function point analysis* (FPA). The intent is to produce a measurement of software size and the process is used to develop the software by evaluating inputs and outputs in terms of both number and complexity. In addition, large applications will utilize a variety of files and interfaces with users as well as external interfaces. These are normally placed in a matrix.

MEASUREMENT PARAMETER	COUNT	WEIGHTING FACTOR			
		SIMPLE	AVERAGE	COMPLEX	RESULTS
Number of user inputs	X3	4	6		
Number of user outputs	X4	5	7		
Number of user inquiries	X3	4	6		
Number of files	X7	10	15		
Number of external interfaces	X5	7	10		
Count Total					

It should be noted that, although CISA candidates are expected to be aware of the use of FPA as an indirect measurement of the software size, candidates will not be examined on how to perform the calculation.

Project Tracking and Oversight

The overall objective of project tracking and oversight is to provide adequate visibility of actual progress so that the management can take effective actions when the project's performance appears to deviate significantly from the original plans. Despite the best planning process, any project is vulnerable to poor execution. In addition, the longer the project duration, the more likely it is that the original business objective will deviate from its initial intention. Oversight and tracking throughout all phases of the development process help ensure that control is maintained, and standard processes are followed. Oversight and tracking controls are essential to identify projects which are deviating from original planning objectives and performance indicators.

Project Management Tools

Accurate project scheduling techniques have long been a goal in any project management. Internal auditing frequently works in project teams, which often suffer from the same poor project scheduling.

Many of the quantitative tools such as GANTT charts, PERT charts, and critical path analysis are used by management to control time and budgets. Overall, the management areas of planning, leading, and controlling remain fundamental to the project management process.

GANTT or Bar Charts

One of the simplest planning tools requiring no mathematical calculations is the GANTT chart. It is commonly used in organizing work and monitoring progress through the various stages of a simple project and involves the production of bar charts showing the start and completion times of individual project activities. The major drawback to these charts is the poorer representation of interdependencies.

Program Evaluation Review Techniques (Also Known as a Network Diagram)

The program evaluation review technique (PERT) is used to diagrammatically identify dependent and independent activities. By showing graphically which activities cannot be started until the previous activities have been completed and, at the same time, which activities can proceed simultaneously, the planner can allocate resources to those tasks having the most impact on the final completion deadline. This technique also takes into consideration operational constraints placed on the resources needed to carry out the tasks as can be seen in the example:

a) Path A–B–C–D–E takes eight days.
b) Path A–F–G–D–E takes four days.
c) Path A–H–I–E takes nine days.

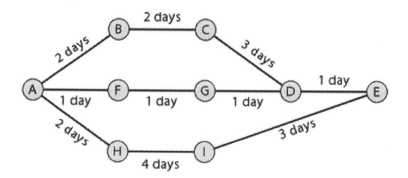

In a PERT chart, the shortest time to get from start to finish while completing all tasks is calculated by calculating the longest path. As such, in the above example, path c) would be the critical path such that any delay in any of these activities will delay the final delivery of the project. By the same token, path b) can afford a limited (four day) delay in its activities without affecting the final delivery date. Any delay exceeding the four-day limit would effectively turn path b) into the critical path. PERT charts are commonly used for projects where the time needed to complete different activities is not known and can only be estimated. There are three times estimates used in PERT:

- Optimistic time
- Most likely time
- Pessimistic time

This compares to the two estimates used in the critical path method (CPM).

Critical Path Method

The critical path method (CPM) is a scheduling tool that was developed independently of PERT but uses a similar diagram. CPM, however, uses two time estimates: one for normal effort and one for 'crash' effort. 'Crash' time is the time required for completion if all available resources were committed to that task.

Project management software is commonly used to allow project managers to produce plans and forecasts in graphical, easy-to-read formats, to plot deadlines, and share documents. Project management software can help project teams handle common problems, such as slipped deadlines, by automatically rescheduling tasks they are involved in. These tools may be provided as online services or within standalone software, and some are available as either freeware or shareware. It is a question of selecting the appropriate tool for the project framework selected.

Timebox Management

Timeboxing is a time management technique commonly used in prototype development. In all rapid application development approaches the real intention is to deliver key features a short time frame.

In this approach a planned activity is allocated a fixed time period. The activity is worked on for the duration of the fixed time period and work on it ceases at the end of the time period. At that point an assessment is made regarding the planned goals for the activity. Key features of this approach include the development of interfaces for future integrations. This approach is intended to prevent project cost overruns and schedule delays and has the added benefit that it facilitates the monitoring of achievement both of individuals and teams. It also allows the integration of system testing and user acceptance testing as they are commonly performed together.

Management of Resource Usage

Resource usage refers to the process by which the project budget is being spent. Measurement of resource usage facilitates whether resources are being utilized as intended through measurement and reporting.

A common technique in this arena is *Earned Value Analysis* (EVA). This involves the identification of appropriate metrics such as actual spending to date compared to a budget to date and estimate to completion.

Auditor's Role in the Project Management Process

In auditing the process, the auditor's traditional role is to evaluate whether the controls within the project management are adequate to provide reasonable assurance that the system will be delivered as required and that the appropriate business control processes have been incorporated into the design of the new or amended system. The auditor's objectives are thus two-fold, namely to ensure that the controls over a significant corporate investment in the development of systems will produce value-for-money and, at the same time, to ensure that systems developed meet the internal control requirements of the business.

In achieving the latter, the auditor may undertake the role of being a part of the systems development process. This is often seen as a hindrance to auditor independence but should rather be regarded as the auditor, as the most appropriate person, undertaking the role of internal control consultant. The individual auditor's independence may be compromised, but another auditor, auditing independently, should find a system with well-designed controls incorporated. This role may mean that, during the development process, the auditor may be required to participate in the selected project management meetings in addition to risk assessment, systems design, development, and systems delivery meetings in order to provide ongoing, proactive control recommendations. All of these tasks may be appropriate for the auditor in a consultancy role.

An alternate role for the auditor is the review of end-stage deliverables throughout the development process without becoming a part of the process. In this role, the auditor will review each stage's deliverables in order to ensure that what was planned from the previous stage has been accomplished, and that the planning of the next stage has been refined appropriately.

Either role will require that the auditor acquires an in-depth understanding of both the overall IT development processes adopted within the organization and the business process being computerized. The audit will result in the production of formal audit reports to the appropriate business managers including an overall assessment of the controlled progress of the project as well as areas requiring improvement in order to complete the project, as specified, within budget and at an appropriate quality.

Audit Risk Assessment

Risk analysis involves estimating the significance of the risk and assessing the likelihood or frequency of the risk. Management and auditors must consider how the risk should be managed, what actions need to be taken, and what controls need to be affected. Should they be *preventative* procedures to reduce the significance or likelihood of the risk occurring or *displacement* procedures to offset the impact if it does occur? Risks are normally evaluated before considering the mitigating effects of controls in order to establish *inherent risk*. Inherent risk may be defined as the gross risk of a specific threat ignoring risk reduction elements. It becomes an informed, subjective evaluation of maximum risk. Within this context, *control risk* may be seen as that portion of inherent risk not covered by a single control element. That is the net exposure after a given control is accounted for. Taken collectively, *control structure risk* may be seen as an informed, subjective evaluation of the maximum potential net exposure after assessing the full control structure.

Process analysis is the procedure that permits the identification of key dependencies and control nodes and looks at the processes within a business entity. It identifies cross-organizational dependencies, such as where business data originates, where it is stored, how it is converted to useful information, and who uses the information. Quality control programs can positively affect these business processes. Risk factors may be unique to each organization and must be determined by a risk assessment.

In identifying threats, a threat itself is an event that will result in direct damage unless averted or mitigated by controls. These should be identified by mixed discipline teams consisting of:

- System users
- Information System staff
- Auditors

Risk analysis is a far from foolproof technique and has inherent limitations, such as poor judgment in decision making, or access may not be available to data that is complete, accurate, or timely. People make wrong decisions or get tired and make mistakes. Collusion (two or more people acting together) can occur. Management override that bypasses the system of internal control may be possible.

Meaningful risk analysis can substantially increase the probability of achieving project objectives, since it alerts management to changes needed to project control procedures and links activity objectives to action. Risk analysis focuses effort on control procedures and should become second nature. The process may be formal or informal; however, it is the results, not the degree of formality, that matter.

Common tasks may include activities such as:

- Conducting meetings with key project team members focusing upon the critical components of the system in order to determine the areas that require controls to ensure business objectives and user requirements are achieved.
- Discussing the alternative control opportunities with project team members, both from the user perspective and the IT systems, in order to determine the mission critical risks to and exposures of the system.

- Evaluating the adequacy of existing controls and advise the stakeholders regarding the adequacy of the design of the system of internal controls.
- Reviewing the documentation and deliverables used to monitor the systems development process to ensure that designed controls are implemented and that the desired development/acquisition methodology is being followed.
- Reviewing and evaluating application system audit trails to ensure that documented controls are in place to address all security, edit, and processing controls.
- Evaluating test plans to ensure defined system requirements are being verified.
- Tracking information in a change management system.
- Evaluating the adequacy of production library security to ensure the integrity of the production systems.
- Examining audit evidence such as test results to evaluate the system maintenance process to ensure control objectives continue to be achieved.
- Reviewing the adequacy of documentation.
- Participating as required in post-implementation reviews.

Audit Planning

Internal Auditors should note that IIA Practice Advisory 2010-2: Linking the Audit Plan to Risk and Exposures guides an internal auditor in linking the internal audit plan to the assessment of risk and exposures that may affect the business.

> The internal audit activity's audit plan should be designed based on an assessment of risk and exposures that may affect the organization. Ultimately, key audit objectives are to provide management with information to mitigate the negative consequences associated with accomplishing the organization's objectives, as well as an assessment of the effectiveness of management's risk management activities. The degree or materiality of exposure can be viewed as risk mitigated by establishing control activities.[*]

---

[*] IIA Practice Advisory 2010-2: Linking the Audit Plan to Risk and Exposures

Selling the risk-based audit approach involves obtaining management buy-in to the process. One effective way of achieving this is to ensure all stakeholders participate in both risk identification and risk evaluation.

In order for the project to achieve its desired objectives, *appropriate project management* will be required, utilizing a variety of management skills and disciplines as well as the implementation of appropriate tools and techniques. Project management is generally accepted as comprising six specific elements:

- Project initiation
- Project planning
- Project execution
- Project monitoring
- Project controlling
- Project closing

Project initiation involves scoping the audit based on the criteria established in conjunction with the user and management, encompassing the control objectives of the system user, potential risks and exposures, and a selection of the appropriate forms the audit should take. From this an approximation of the size and composition of the audit team may be established.

Project planning involves the breaking down of the audit into specific tasks to be achieved, allocating work to individuals, and determining the timing and overlaps of specific audit phases. Planning techniques such as the use of the GANTT charts, CPM, and the like may come into play, and scheduling of the work. At this stage budget and cost estimates can be prepared, taking into consideration the logistics of the audit. Planning will also involve the selection of the appropriate monitoring techniques to be enacted during the audit execution.

Project execution will involve the audit team leader in ensuring that the whole audit process is directed towards the achievement of the scope and objectives initially established. This normally involves monitoring progress against the plan and, where deviations occur, modifying the plan in order to put the project back online.

Project monitoring is traditionally done by monitoring time spent against plan, although this may not be the most effective way of project management. Rather, monitoring against predetermined key indicators established at the end of critical audit components may be more appropriate.

Project controlling involves the lead auditor maintaining the group focus, control, and quality of work done and ensuring that unforeseen circumstances or risks do not inadvertently obstruct the completion of the audit.

Project closing can be as difficult for audit as for any other project. The temptation exists to 'just check one more thing', resulting in a significant deviation from the scope, timing, costing, and quality of the overall audit. It is part of the role of the lead auditor to bring the project to a successful conclusion, evaluate, and discuss with the team the successes, failures, and learning points of the audit, and determine which conclusions and evidence will be communicated onwards via the audit report.

The lead auditor's role is to ensure that, ultimately, the audit project achieves its objective. This involves establishing clear objectives for the audit project and organizing resources to provide adequate assurance that the objectives will be achieved within acceptable quality, cost, and time constraints. Periodically, unforeseen circumstances will place competing demands on resource availability for the audit project, and this will then involve adjustments to the audit approach, timing, and possibly even the scope of the audit.

An audit of the project management process would involve the assessment of the adequacy of the control environment utilized for managing projects. Auditors will seek to determine both the status of the project's internal control system and the status of the development project itself. These process audits eliminate the necessity of devoting large amounts of audit resources to the development effort itself. By ensuring the development process is well controlled, the need for audit involvement in the process itself is minimized.

Domain 2 – Practice Questions

1. IT architectures will:
   a. Change constantly to ensure the best approach is taken to satisfy user requirements.
   b. Remain unchanged to ensure standardization of approach.
   c. Change occasionally as technology changes.

    d. Remain unchanged as it is independent of technology and requirements.

2. A project may be defined as:
    a. An undertaking involving multiple individuals.
    b. An undertaking involving common techniques to develop a standardized product.
    c. A temporary endeavor undertaken to accomplish a unique purpose.
    d. Involving only the development of new software.

3. Project control is designed to:
    a. Maximize the likelihood of successful outcomes.
    b. Minimize the risk of non-achievement of objectives.
    c. Eliminate delivery-risk.
    d. Control the consumption of resources.

4. The most critical component of project management is:
    a. An effective project manager.
    b. An effective project plan.
    c. Effectively monitoring deliverables.
    d. A constant audit presence.

5. Archibald's six phases include:
    a. Concept, development, and audit.
    b. Concept, definition, and audit.
    c. Development, definition, and audit.
    d. Concept, development, and definition.

6. In a *waterfall* cycle:
    a. The cycle starts with the development of a baseline product then moves through several iterations.
    b. Each activity cascades from the previous activity.
    c. Business strategy dictates the formulation of explicit user requirements.
    d. Audit is the verification stage, which may be deemed complete when the system can meet the functional, operational, and control stipulations of the detailed business specification.

7. Product quality is a measurement of:
   a. The degree to which customer needs and expectations are satisfied.
   b. Efficiency and effectiveness of the process which creates the end product.
   c. The economy and efficiency of the process which creates the end product.
   d. The degree to which customers' expectations are exceeded.

8. Performance measurement may be seen as:
   a. A methodology of offering feed-forward mechanisms to ensure continued quality of programs and services.
   b. An environment in which operational plans provide information to top executives.
   c. A methodology to prevent changes in both internal and external environments.
   d. An iterative process involving the setting of objectives, development of plans and strategies to achieve those objectives, and development of progress measurements to assess progress towards its objectives.

9. A balanced scorecard involves measuring:
   a. Financial performance.
   b. Client satisfaction and internal business processes.
   c. The degree of innovation and learning.
   d. All of the above.

10. Performance measurement using a *one size fits all* approach:
   a. Is inappropriate due to the extreme variations in architectures, methodologies, and approaches undertaken in developing and utilizing information systems.
   b. Is appropriate due to the extreme variations in architectures, methodologies, and approaches undertaken in developing and utilizing information systems.
   c. Is inappropriate due to the varying skill levels of individuals involved.
   d. Is appropriate due to the varying skill levels of individuals involved.

11. Outsourcing of information system services is normally chosen when:
    a. The cost of in-house processing is low.
    b. The risks associated with executor function is determined to be too high to outsource.
    c. The organization does not have sufficient competence to tackle the work itself.
    d. All of the above.

12. At the end of a five-year development program, the new information system was found not to achieve current corporate objectives. This most likely resulted from:
    a. Poor initial alignment of IS and organizational strategies.
    b. Failure of change management.
    c. Lack of flexibility in the final system.
    d. Poor quality assurance in the development process.

13. Achieving information processing cost reduction is an indication of:
    a. Efficiency.
    b. Effectiveness.
    c. Value for money.
    d. Flexibility.

14. Evaluation of IT planning would typically involve Audit looking at:
    a. Organization design.
    b. Span of control.
    c. IT command structures.
    d. Forecasting of needs and requirements.

15. Using a steering committee has the primary objective of:
    a. Ensuring no single individual can be blamed for failure.
    b. Providing a discussion medium where all opinions can be aired.
    c. Bringing diverse skills and perspectives to bear on the alignment of the IS strategy.
    d. To ensure that interventions result in low-cost systems.

16. COBIT® may be defined as:
    a. Part of ISO 9000.
    b. An attempt to blend existing IT standards into one comprehensive structure.
    c. Mandatory for all IT sites.
    d. Limited to IS security only.

17. 'Best practices' may be described as:
    a. Practices appropriate to an organization based on its needs and capabilities.
    b. Practices performed by the best companies in an area.
    c. Mandatory for all IT sites.
    d. Essential to achieve adequate standards.

18. COBIT® is designed to be utilized by:
    a. Different levels of management.
    b. IT management.
    c. Audit management.
    d. User management.

19. The process of change control may include:
    a. Hardware only.
    b. Software only.
    c. Application software only.
    d. All of the above.

20. Changes may be required as a result of:
    a. Failures during normal operations.
    b. Changes to legislation.
    c. Changes to the business operation of the organization.
    d. All of the above.

21. Change control is required to ensure all of the below except:
    a. All changes are audited.
    b. All changes are authorized.
    c. All authorized changes are made.
    d. Only authorized changes are made.

22. IS auditors sign off on changes in order to:
    a. Indicate that audits control requirements have been met.
    b. Indicate that all testing has been done.

    c. Indicate that the change control process has been effective.

    d. All of the above.

23. Threats to integrity and privacy from inside the organization include:

    a. Loss or destruction of assets by malicious acts.

    b. Errors from incompetence or carelessness.

    c. Deliberate exposure of private or privileged information.

    d. All of the above.

Domain 2 – Review Questions and Hands-on Exercise

- Define the components of the management of an IS infrastructure and alternative IS architecture configuration.
- Define the functions involved in IS project management.
- Define what is required in software quality control management.
- Explain what is required in order to manage IS delivery (operations) and support (maintenance).
- Explain the components of performance measurement and reporting: IS balanced scorecard.
- Define control risks and opportunities in outsourcing.
- Describe in define the audit indicators.
- Define Cloud computing and its effect on Risk Management.
- Define the process for the development, deployment, and maintenance of the IS strategy.
- Describe the policies and procedures as well as standards and processes utilized to support the IS strategy.
- Describe the components of the IS/IT strategic planning: competitive strategies and business intelligence, link to corporate strategy.
- Define the types of strategic information systems frameworks and applications: types of IS, knowledge management, decision support systems; classification of information systems.

Exercise 2 – Audit of Customer Receivables

The current accounting system has developed over a period of years. The documentation of the system is limited, and the individual who developed most of the system has recently retired. The employees seem very well trained and appear to be capable. The replacement for the retired system developer has a limited knowledge of the system's capabilities and controls. The original system manual, flow charts, and so forth are in the department's office, but are badly out of date.

- Transaction data is captured from several sources. Most of the transactions are billings and payments for clothing and are entered electronically from a variety of interfacing systems. A key control for this process involves verifying customer numbers for validity and accuracy, and matching invoice data to the purchase data recorded. The invoices are processed in real time and the computer verification is heavily relied on to help ensure the accuracy and completeness of the processing.
- The individual stores around the country, as well as other functions at head office, can input transactions electronically. Suspense files capture the transactions that are rejected by the receivable system. Because these departments were outside the scope of the audit, they were not examined.
- The cashier processes cash payments from customers. Since this is a treasury function, it was also considered to be outside the scope of the customer receivables audit. The transactions from the cashier are electronically transmitted to the customer accounts receivable program, and suspense files capture transactions that are not acceptable.

The auditors relied solely upon discussions with management and users and did not look at the system documentation or further test the system.

You are required to:

From the information above, identify the business and special risks associated with the current system. Briefly justify why these are business risks to the organization.

Exercise 2 Sample Answer

Business risks include:

- Failure to account for all sales resulting in poor recovery of revenues
- Failure to understand the needs of customers resulting in failure to attract new customers and loss of existing customers as well as overstocking of slow-moving goods
- Ineffective billing of customers and erroneous billing of potential customers may result in loss of customers and failure to attract new ones
- Poor management of credit risk resulting in significant losses to the organization through the granting of credit to non-creditworthy customers
- Failure to achieve superlative customer service will result in loss of customers to competitive stores

Special risks could include:

- Technology not performing as predicted
- Risks associated with system interfaces – loss of transactions, duplication, fraud etc.
- Non-availability of technology
- Staff unfamiliar with technology
- Discrepancies between large stores and smaller stores operating procedures

Domain 2 – Answers to Practice Questions

1. **A** The primary objective of the IT architecture is to ensure principles, guidelines, and rules used by an enterprise to direct the overall process of acquiring, building, modifying, and interfacing IT resources across the enterprise are effective. This may involve modification as overall user requirements change over a period of time.

2. **C** Projects are, by their nature, template undertakings established to accomplish a specific objective and may involve one or more individuals using a variety of techniques to develop a potentially unique product. Projects may involve the development of new software or modification of existing software.

3. **B** Project control is a management exercise intended to minimize the risk of a particular project failing to achieve as overall objectives.

4. **A** As with most management exercises, the effectiveness of management itself is a primary prerequisite. B) and C) would both be part of the management process while a constant audit presence would not be a prerequisite.

5. **D** Archibald's six phases include: Concept, Definition, Design, Development, Application, and Post-Completion. Audit is not part of the six phases.

6. **B** In a waterfall cycle each activity 'cascades' from the previous activity to lead ultimately to fully deployed information systems.

7. **A** The effectiveness of the product is indicated by the degree to which customer needs and expectations are satisfied. Exceeding customer expectations is not a requisite. Answers B) and C) refer to the process rather than the product.

8. **D** Performance measurement is a process rather than a methodology or referring to the environment.

9. **D** A balanced scorecard involves measuring client satisfaction, financial performance, and the degree of innovation and learning.

10. **A** One size fits all is inappropriate in measuring performance because of the wide variations in architectures methodologies and approaches.

11. **C** The prime reason for outsourcing information system services is lack of sufficient competence within the organization itself to tackle the work.

12. **A** While B) and C) may result in a five-year development program not achieving current corporate objectives, the most common reason for such failure is poor alignment at the start of the project.

13. **D** Cost control is a factor of efficiency, effectiveness, and value for money, but achieving cost reduction is a common indication of flexibility in the process.

14. **C** IT planning is dictated via the command structures and is generally the first place for audit investigation.

15. **C** While steering committees do provide a medium where all opinions can be aired, the intention of the steering committee is to allow diverse skills and perspectives to be brought to bear

on the alignment of the IS strategy. Neither cost nor avoidance of blame is at fault.

16. **B** COBIT® may be defined as an attempt to blend existing IT standards into a single comprehensive structure. It is not compulsory for all IT sites and it is not confined to security only. Nor is it part of ISO 9000 which is an international quality standard not specifically for information systems.

17. **B** 'Best practices' is a term used to compare current organizational practices with the best companies operating in the same area.

18. **A** COBIT® is intended to be utilized by varying levels of management in order to achieve a unique system of internal controls specifically tailored to the business needs of the organization.

19. **D** Change control applies equally to hardware, application software, and system software.

20. **D** Changes may come about as a result of operational failures as well as changes to the business operations of the organization or to legislation.

21. **A** The requirement that all changes be audited is not part of the change control mechanism.

22. **B** IS auditors will sign off on changes in order to indicate that evidence is been seen that all testing has been done as per organizational standards.

23. **D** Errors from incompetence or carelessness, malicious acts, and deliberate exposure of private or privileged information may all arise within the organization.

4

DOMAIN 3 – INFORMATION SYSTEMS ACQUISITION, DEVELOPMENT, AND IMPLEMENTATION

This chapter covers the processes involved in the acquisition, development, testing, and implementation of information systems to meet the organization's strategies and objectives.

As has been noted, this domain comprises approximately 18% of the examination, that is some 27 questions. Seven tasks and 14 knowledge statements are included within this domain.

Systems Acquisition

In order to meet the changing needs of today's business environments, organizations have to plan for the long term and this includes the acquisition of information systems and services that will support business initiatives and interventions. This includes acting in a responsible manner to emerging opportunities created both within IT systems and external to the organization. As part of the ongoing business planning process the need for new and revised application systems must be determined as well as the prioritization and the setting of appropriate time scales.

When the strategic planning indicates a need for a specific information system the acquisition process starts. This process is normally carried out in order to facilitate the integration of new or revised systems into the overall information systems architecture already in place. Such acquisition may rely on the development or modification of systems internally or external acquisition from a third party.

In general, software can be acquired as a package and tailored for the organization or developed specifically to meet the unique needs of the purchaser.

Purchasing or leasing software from a software company or vendor, as opposed to developing it in-house, is an attractive alternative for many organizations and offers a number of advantages, including:

- Lower costs
- Less risk
- High quality
- Less time
- Fewer resources needed

It should not be imagined that the acquisition of a packaged solution completely removes the need for corporate involvement in the process. Using an externally developed, purchased program involves more than just paying for the package. Certain acts are still needed and the following steps are suggested:

- Review needs and requirements
- Select vendor
- Acquire software
- Modify or customize software
- Acquire or develop software interfaces
- User testing and acceptance
- Maintenance and modifications

Care should be taken to ensure that the organization is not defining requirements for features that will never be used but that could significantly add to the costs and time schedule. Installation and tuning of the most standard packages take time and effort and should not be underestimated. By the same token, future modifications will undoubtedly be required, and the cost and ease of maintenance must be considered. The initial stage within the systems acquisition is the issuing of a *Request for Information* (RFI). Information about potential vendor products may already be available but, by using a formal RFI, data can be gathered not only on the product but on the overall desirability of doing business with this particular vendor.

At this stage detailed analysis of the intended functional capabilities may not have been performed and may eventually include information drawn as a result of the RFI document. In order for a supplier to adequately complete an RFI, certain information must be provided including an overview of the organization, the outline functionality desired, and the operational environment (hardware and systems software) currently in place as well as any existing application systems with which interfaces must be developed.

One danger in this approach is that the subsequent detailed requirements definition may be colored by the project team's awareness of the functional capabilities of specific packages, which could potentially bias selection criteria.

The *Detailed Requirements Definition* phase defines the functional requirements of the proposed system in sufficient detail to facilitate selection of the appropriate vendor package. This document defines the business requirements of the proposed system together with the business controls to be effected within the new system. At this stage, technical specifications may or may not be included. Where there are known technical constraints, it would be expected that these be detailed within the definition, particularly if there are predetermined hardware and/or software requirements. User involvement at this stage is critical as is that of the IT auditor to ensure all operational requirements and control requirements are covered. Where one or more packages meet the requirements defined within the definition document, a *Request for Proposal* (RPF) will be sent to the vendor to elicit bids for any or all of: delivery, tailoring, and implementation of the packaged solution. This document is based upon the requirements definition document but should also include information on the user base to be supported by the system and a description of the operational environment within which the system will operate.

Once a selection has been made and the contracts have been agreed and signed, the expectation is that the package will be delivered and the installation will happen as a matter of course. The reality is that the installation, even of a package solution, must be planned carefully in order to ensure a smooth implementation in the same way as an in-house developed system.

Cloud-Based Systems Acquisition

Increasingly, organizations are using cloud computing to deliver Software as a Service (SaaS). Increasingly SaaS is seen as a cost-effective way to acquire systems on an on-demand basis. Companies gain the advantages of scalability and the avoidance of capital expenditures and using public clouds. In acquiring SaaS, the enterprise may elect to a lease of propriety package from a vendor and have it customized by the vendor or internally. Alternatively, the company may choose to employ an open source application where the program code is freely available and open to modification by the organization or third party of the company's choice. The cloud environment generally offers the organization flexibility and guaranteed resource availability in addition to potential cost savings. The disadvantage in the use of public clouds may lie in the partial loss of direct control.

Even within cloud computing firms may choose to implement their own private clouds in order to share resources for employee use across the network. These include environments dedicated to the exclusive use of the organization. Traditionally, private clouds ran in-house and behind the user's firewall. Increasingly private clouds are being built on vendor-owned data centers located externally. In either event, the primary control benefits of private clouds include the strength of security and demonstrable regulatory compliance which can be implemented.

Systems Development

Systems development is part of a life cycle process with pre-defined phases applicable to deployment, maintenance, and retirement of application systems. Each individual phase forms the basis for the next step.

There are two primary categories of application systems:

Where the objective of an application is to provide different views of data for their performance optimization it may be referred to as an *End-User-Centric* system.

Requirements for new business applications are frequently derived from:

- Problems existing within current business processes, technology, or application systems
- The advent of new technology facilitating new business opportunities
- The need to align business processes or applications with trends or movements and industry standards or Data Processing business partners

The systems are frequently developed using alternative development methodologies rather than the standard SDLC.

The other application systems category relates to those applications designed to facilitate the sharing of information with users across a variety of applications support functions based on their need-to-know. These *Organization–Centric* systems, are designed to collect information, store, and archive the data, and facilitate cross-functional sharing.

Such an application development that typically uses the formal SDLC process and is derived from the needs of individual business functions, tailored to fit the overall strategic goals of the organization. This form of development is commonly utilized with objectives that fall into the five *SMART* criteria *(Specific, Measurable, Attainable, Relevant, and Timely)* so that prioritization and progress may be measured using quantifiable indicators.

The SDLC

IT systems development normally follows a standardized development cycle. Partly because of the special challenges posed by the intangible nature of software, and the importance of getting user involvement in a structured manner, this process tends to be both consistent and dominant.

There are various versions of this: the spiral, the waterfall, and the vee. In his definitive work in 1976, Archibald[*] defined the project life cycle as having identifiable start and end points and passing through six distinct phases, namely:

1. Concept
2. Definition
3. Design
4. Development
5. Application
6. Post-completion

---

[*] R. D. Archibald, *Managing High-Technology Programs and Projects*, Third Edition, 2003. New York: Wiley, p. 19.

This led to the development of the *waterfall* cycle where it can be seen that each activity 'cascades' from the previous activity to lead ultimately to fully deployed information systems. In this model the difference is that the major activities overlap significantly. The major difficulty with this model is software development's need to progress iteratively is not catered for because each project remains with the identifiable start and end points.

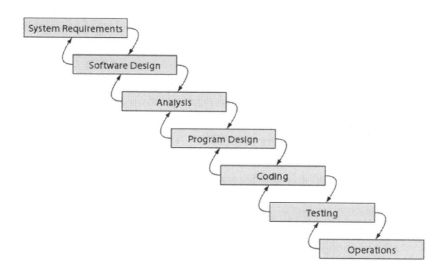

In 1988 Boehm proposed an *iterative spiral* model for the development and enhancement of computer software.[*] Boehm's spiral involved four major functions, namely:

- Next stage planning
- Determining objectives, alternatives, and constraints/evaluation of alternatives
- Identifying and resolving risk issues
- Developing and verifying the next level product

These functions commence with the development of a baseline product and then move through several iterations until the final product is implemented.

---

[*] B. Boehm, 'A Spiral Model of Software Development and Enhancement.' IEEE Computer (May 1988): 61–72.

An alternative development based upon the waterfall cycle was suggested by Fish[*] and is known as the *vee* cycle, and it follows a sequence such as that shown below:

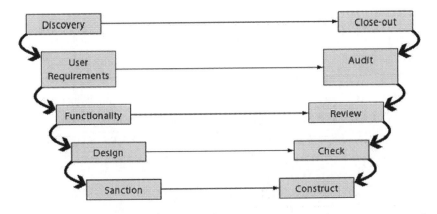

Business strategy dictates the formulation of business require-ments, which will usually incorporate explicit user requirements. These then lead to the definition of systems requirements and speci-fications. These allow the formation of the architectural design of the software and coding then creates the individual components of the system, which is then tested 'up' the waterfall against the different levels of specification. From a control and audit perspective this form of systems development is considered the easier to audit because at each level there are standards to match against as well as the existence of a separate audit stage.

Within an IT environment, the Vee approach would typically involve:

- *Discovery* is the point in the process when the IT or user area finds there is a market for a specific system. This phase is brief; there are few decisions to be made.
- *Requirement* is when the user can write an outline system specification that states: 'We need a system capable of the following functionality A, B, C ...' At this stage a feasibility study may include an assessment of the technical feasibility of this system, its costs, and potential benefits.

---

[*] E. Fish, An Improved Project Lifecycle Model, Pandora Consulting, http://www.maxwideman.com/guests/plc/intro.htm (Guest Department), 2002, updated 2003.

- *Functionality* is when the user can write a detailed business specification that states all of the business, operational, and control requirements. At this stage the feasibility study may be revisited to reassess the technical feasibility of this system, its costs, and potential benefits.

- *Design* results in the detailed system specification that specifies file layouts, screen design, the required hardware and software environment, networking requirements, and any potential limitations or requirements for new hardware and software to be acquired.

- *Sanction* is the phase wherein board approval for design and expenditure is sought prior to the commitment of resources to the longest part of the process.

- *Construct* is the purchase or development of the software including the coding, unit-testing, and documentation of the application systems.

- *Check* is used to verify that what is installed is what was intended to be installed as set out in the design documents. Also, that installation was done according to those design documents.

- *Review* involves testing subsystems, usually with a test material to ensure that the intention of the system has been met. This phase tests collections of hardware and software (systems) against the design intent and the interaction of integrated systems.

- *Audit* is the verification stage, which may be deemed to be complete when the system can meet the functional, operational, and control stipulations of the detailed business specification.

- *Close-out* is the stage wherein the cycle is completed by ensuring the installed product matches the need identified during the discovery phase.

As can be seen from this model, the left-hand side of the vee shows the planning stages, while the right-hand side indicates the implementation or 'doing' stages.

Over and above the methodology selected, project managers require competencies in multiple areas. From a task management perspective they need to be able to manage the project *scope, cost, duration,* and *quality*. At the same time they need to be able to manage their human resources with good communications while simultaneously ensuring risk is controlled and that the whole project is adequately integrated.

Many of the quantitative tools such as Gantt charts, PERT charts, and critical path analysis are used by management to control time and budgets. Overall, the management areas of planning, leading, and controlling remain fundamental to the development process.

The Iterative Model

This model is a cyclical process whereby individual business requirements are developed and tested in a series of iterations until the full application has been designed, constructed, and tested. For each iteration the full SDLC is used for each phase.

Prototyping and Rapid Application Development (RAD)

An alternative to the traditional development process involves the use of rapid development techniques such as prototyping or rapid application development techniques. These involve the rapid transformation of the user's essential requirements into a basic working model followed by the revision and enhancement of the model ultimately leading to the decision to accept the model as the final simulation of the actual system to be built.

The prototype model facilitates interaction between the users, system analysts, and the auditor and allows models to be reviewed and analyzed before the commitment of large funding for systems development. Increased user and audit participation in the design of the project will normally increase the acceptability of the final system and systems maintenance requirements are normally reduced due, again, to early user involvement. Unfortunately, this early involvement can lead to a user perception that the system is 'nearly complete' at an early stage of development potentially resulting in ineffective implementations.

Agile Methodologies

Agile methodologies utilize incremental changes with each increment being released in a specific period of time (time box) allowing a regular release schedule. Agile methodologies are based on the Agile Manifesto first released in 2001, with the following the basic principles:

- Our highest priority is to satisfy the customer through early and continuous delivery of valuable software.
- Welcome changing requirements, even late in development. Agile processes harness change for the customer's competitive advantage.
- Deliver working software frequently, from a couple of weeks to a couple of months, with a preference to the shorter timescale.
- Business people and developers must work together daily throughout the project.
- Build projects around motivated individuals.
- Give them the environment and support they need, and trust them to get the job done.
- The most efficient and effective method of conveying information to and within a development team is face-to-face conversation.
- Working software is the primary measure of progress.
- Agile processes promote sustainable development.
- The sponsors, developers, and users should be able to maintain a constant pace indefinitely.
- Continuous attention to technical excellence and good design enhances agility.
- Simplicity – the art of maximizing the amount of work not done – is essential.
- The best architectures, requirements, and designs emerge from self-organizing teams.
- At regular intervals, the team reflects on how to become more effective, then tunes and adjusts its behavior accordingly.*

Such methodologies typically include small, cross-functional teams incorporating representatives from both IT and the user community with frequent status meetings and short time-frame increments for completion of each phase.

---

* http://agilemanifesto.org/principles.html

Lean Methodology

The basic concept of this methodology is to take the initial idea and develop a *minimum viable product* (MVP). This is defined as a working software application with just enough functionality to prove the idea behind the project. The MVP is then given to potential users for review in order to determine whether the project should continue, be amended, or whether a new MVP should be created. This technique is common where the organization seeks to determine whether the original idea for the software application is worth developing.

Systems Implementation

In the case of the installation of packages, there is frequently a requirement for some programming of interfaces and customization of the package. As with any other programming this must follow the traditional life cycle including the appropriate analysis, design, programming, and testing phases. Data acquisition and conversion programs must also be planned and, where necessary, data must be sanitized (cleaned-up) prior to conversion into the new system.

Where the system is being developed internally, and regardless of the development methodology selected. Implementation itself typically involves:

- Programming
- Coding
- Prototyping
- Unit testing
- Test linking to other modules
- Documentation
- Installation
- User acceptance testing
- Parallel running
- User training
- File conversion
- Live running

Testing of systems is a complex business involving programmers, systems analysts, users, and internal auditors. The first three must satisfy themselves that the system performs as desired in that it does everything it is supposed to and conversely does NOT do the things it is not supposed to. The auditor's role is to satisfy himself that the testing has, in fact, been done and been done to acceptable standards.

Once the system has been developed and adequately tested, conversion from the previous manual/computer system must take place. This will typically involve:

- Acquisition of data
- Identification of sources
- Development of conversion programs
- Sanitization of input data
- File conversion

System conversion is a major task and requires that strict control be enforced. Audit involvement is essential at this stage but care should be taken to ensure that audit's role does not become one of IT quality assurance. The auditor's role is to ensure that management has adequate controls to ensure that conversion was effective.

While all this is going on, maintenance must continue on the current systems.

Systems Maintenance Review

Systems maintenance review is the process of analyzing existing systems to ensure they are operating as intended and may be event or time driven. Factors to be considered in conducting systems reviews include:

- Response time
- Training
- Reliability
- Mission
- Goals and objectives
- Procedures
- Communications
- Hardware and software
- IS personnel
- IS budgets

- Efficiency
- Documentation

Such reviews involve a critical evaluation of all systems components. This would include not only the software but also any databases, telecommunications, personnel, and procedures.

Systems maintenance involves checking, changing, and enhancing the system to make it more useful in obtaining user and organization goals.

Once the system has been created, it is essential that it remains intact and impossible to change in an unauthorized or uncontrolled manner. The process of achieving this is called *Change Control*. Change Control's objective is to ensure risk is controlled, not introduced, during a change. This means ensuring that:

- All changes are authorized
- All authorized changes are made
- Only authorized changes are made
- All changes are as specified
- All changes are cost-effective

The changes thus controlled are known and planned changes. The procedures involve ensuring prior authorization for all changes, supervision of the change process, adequate testing of all changes, and user sign-off on all changes.

Normal systems maintenance involves checking, changing, and enhancing the system to make it more useful in obtaining user and organizational goals. Major causes of program maintenance include:

- New requests from users and managers
- Bugs or errors in the program
- Technical and hardware problems
- Corporate mergers and acquisitions
- Governmental regulations that require changes in the program

Maintenance may take the form of a patch, a new release, or even a new version. The cost of maintenance can be staggering. For older programs, the total cost of maintenance can be up to five times greater than the original cost of development. The average programmer can spend between 50% and 75% of his or her time on maintaining existing programs as opposed to developing new ones.

From time to time, things will go wrong with a system which requires a repair urgently. Such changes are not known in advance and are commonly executed and permission sought retrospectively. Such changes are controlled using *Problem Management*. Problem Management's objective is to control systems during emergency situations arising from unforeseen changes. Typically this will involve the bypassing of normal control mechanisms and may require direct programmer access to live data. This must be controlled separately and must involve user authorization, even retrospectively.

Domain 3 – Practice Questions

1. Systems may be acquired from:
   a. Computer dealers and distributors.
   b. Time-sharing companies.
   c. Leasing companies.
   d. All of the above.

2. Advantages of buying a computer package as opposed to developing it in-house include all of the following except:
   a. Enhanced management and control of the development process.
   b. Early implementation of the system.
   c. Transfer of risk to the software supplier.
   d. Cost reduction.

3. IS audit should be involved in the process of systems acquisition in order to:
   a. Implement appropriate controls of the acquisition process.
   b. Provide advice and assistance in control aspects.
   c. Reduce overall costs.
   d. Ensure the package is tailored for the organization.

4. Acquiring an externally developed purchased program involves:
   a. Acquiring software, user testing, and systems maintenance.
   b. Programming, user testing, and acquiring software.

c. User testing, systems maintenance, and user selection.

d. User selection, programming, and system testing.

5. A request for information (RFI) is intended to:

 a. Define the functional requirements of the proposed system.

 b. Define access control constraints for the new system.

 c. Gather information on currently available products.

 d. All of the above.

6. A request for proposal (RFP) is intended to:

 a. Define the functional requirements of the proposed system.

 b. Define access control constraints for the new system.

 c. Gather information on currently available products.

 d. Elicit bids from the vendors.

7. The user function role within the requirements definition is to ensure that it:

 a. Accurately and completely reflects the functional requirements for the proposed system.

 b. Incorporates the access control constraints within which the package must operate.

 c. Includes the implementation schedule.

 d. Includes the nature and level of support to be provided together with the associated costs.

8. Response times in the event of a system problem would normally be included in:

 a. The RFI.

 b. The RD.

 c. The RFP.

 d. The proposal.

9. The systems maintenance review is:

 a. Restricted to hardware only.

 b. Restricted to software only.

 c. Used to determine the cost-effectiveness of new systems.

 d. Used to analyze existing systems to ensure they are operating as intended.

10. Factors to be considered in conducting a feasibility study include:
   a. The likelihood of successful implementation.
   b. The programming language the new system.
   c. The extent of documentation required.
   d. The number of sites running a package.

11. Special bridges into existing systems may be required if:
   a. There is no integration.
   b. The degree of integration is high.
   c. The degree of integration is low.
   d. Significant parts of the old system will be retained.

12. Evaluation criteria used within a feasibility study must ensure:
   a. A bias towards in-house developed systems.
   b. A bias towards purchased systems packages.
   c. A bias towards externally developed systems.
   d. A complete lack of bias.

13. Included within the feasibility study should be a section on:
   a. The use of the 'waterfall' methodology for the SDLC.
   b. The availability of resources to carry out the appropriate development or implementation.
   c. The detailed system specification.
   d. The access controls required for the new system.

14. The outcome of the feasibility study could be:
   a. Not to proceed.
   b. To acquire an external system.
   c. To develop a system internally.
   d. Any of the above.

15. Business disruptions anticipated could include:
   a. The need to retrain existing user staff.
   b. The need to retrain existing IS staff.
   c. The need to retrain existing IS audit staff.
   d. The need to retrain all staff.

16. Data conversion and acquisition must ensure:
   a. Programs to convert data from old systems have been developed appropriately.

b. Valid data has been converted accurately and completely.

c. Conversion routines have been fully tested.

d. All data has been re-loaded from scratch.

17. Major control stages in systems development include:

a. System design, system development, and system maintenance.

b. System design, systems development, and system utilization.

c. System design, system maintenance, and system operation.

d. System maintenance, system operation, and system utilization.

18. System models include:

a. Transaction processing systems.

b. Management information systems.

c. Decision support systems.

d. All of the above.

19. The fundamental of information resource management which addresses the value of knowledge to the organization is:

a. Technology management.

b. Strategic management.

c. Functional management.

d. Information management.

20. General control objectives for information processing include:

a. Compliance, confidentiality, and integrity.

b. Accuracy, usefulness, and confidentiality.

c. Low maintenance, accuracy, and completeness.

d. Accuracy, completeness, and usefulness.

21. All transactions are initially and completely recorded is a control objective of:

a. Input.

b. Processing.

c. Output.

d. Programs.

22. Programmed balancing is a common control over:

a. Input.

    b. Processing.

    c. Output.

    d. Programs.

23. Document scanning is a common control over:

    a. Input.

    b. Processing.

    c. Output.

    d. Programs.

24. Programmed balancing is a common control over:

    a. Input.

    b. Processing.

    c. Output.

    d. Programs.

25. User involvement is a common control over:

    a. Input.

    b. Processing.

    c. Output.

    d. Programs.

Domain 3 – Review Questions and Hands-On Exercise

- Explain what goes into the decision taken to make or buy software.
- Define the phases of the systems development process for purchased packages.
- Describe the user's role and the training required.
- Explain the need for maintenance reviews and describe their types.
- Systems may be acquired from the outsourcing decision and the factors around it.
- Describe the role of the feasibility study within the systems development process.
- Explain the user's role and the training required.
- Explain the auditor's role in the feasibility study process.
- Explain the risks and roles in the conversion process.
- Identify the control objectives of specific Business Systems.

- Describe the types of computer assisted audit techniques and their role in systems auditing.

Exercise 3

You have been assigned to conduct an IT audit of your company's computer database system. Through previous work you know that the system includes a centralized database shared by all users. Access to the database is direct by the users through remote terminals and is controlled by the database software system. The IT department includes a manager of operations and a manager of computer programming, both of whom report to the IT director.

The results of your preliminary survey include the following:

1. There are no restrictions regarding the type of transaction or access to the online terminals.
2. All users and IT personnel have access to the extensive system documentation.
3. Before being entered in the user authorization table, user passwords and access codes are established by user management and approved by the manager of computer programming.
4. The manager of computer programming established and controls the database directory. Users approve any changes to data definition.
5. User requests for data are validated by the system against a transactions-conflict matrix to ensure data is transmitted only to authorized users.
6. System access requires the users to input their passwords, and terminal activity logs are maintained.
7. Input data is edited for reasonableness and completeness, transaction control totals are generated, and transaction logs are maintained.
8. Processing control totals are generated and reconciled to changes in the database.
9. Output is reconciled to transaction and input control totals. The resulting reports are printed and placed in a bin outside the IS room for pickup by the users at their convenience.

10. Backup copies of the database are generated daily and stored in the file library area, access to which is restricted to IT personnel.

Required

a. List **TEN** specific audit steps you would include in your audit program to determine whether transaction input is properly authorized.

b. From the results of your preliminary survey, describe **TEN** controls in the system.

c. Evaluate the relative strengths of the general and application controls for the database system.

Exercise 3 Sample Answer

a. Several audit steps that could be included in an audit program to determine if transaction input is properly authorized are as follows:

1. Obtain and review any written procedures describing transaction input operations.

2. Observe the online terminals and ascertain the risk associated with unrestricted access to the terminals.

3. Obtain and review terminal logs for evidence of password/access validation.

4. Determine whether error reports and/or terminal logs are reviewed periodically to uncover unauthorized access attempts.

5. Obtain and review transaction logs to verify their existence and determine if they are reviewed and approved by the user.

6. Attempt to log on to the system with an invalid password.

7. Obtain and review terminal logs to ensure that errors are corrected and that corrected transactions are entered into the system.

8. Review the system documentation concerning the database authorization table.

9. Obtain and review a copy of the transactions-conflict matrix with user and IT management.

10. Review the system documentation concerning the transactions-conflict matrix.
11. Determine whether the transactions-conflict matrix is reviewed periodically for accuracy.
12. Obtain and review the current password assignments with user management.
13. Review the process by which passwords are assigned.
14. Ascertain whether passwords are reviewed and/or changed periodically.
15. Enter test transactions to verify that transactions are edited for reasonableness and completeness.

b. Several controls in the database system apparent from the results of the preliminary survey include the following:
  1. The system has been extensively documented.
  2. The database software maintains a user authorization table.
  3. There is an approval process for passwords.
  4. The database software maintains a transactions-conflict matrix.
  5. User requests for data are validated by the system.
  6. Users must use passwords to log on to the system.
  7. Terminal activity logs are maintained.
  8. Terminal input is edited.
  9. Transaction control totals are developed and reconciled.
  10. Processing control totals are reconciled to changes in the database.
  11. Output is reconciled to transaction control totals.
  12. Backup copies of the database are made daily.

c. The preliminary survey indicates that the general controls are weak while the application controls are, subject to verification of existence and compliance, strong. Specific general control weaknesses indicated include the following:
  1. There is no database administrator who is separate from EDP operations and computer programming.
  2. Access to the terminals is not restricted.
  3. The system documentation is not available on a 'need-to-know' basis only.
  4. Distribution of printed output is uncontrolled. The majority of the items listed in Part (b) above are application

controls. As described there, sufficient controls over input, processing, and output appear to be in existence to warrant a preliminary finding that the application controls are strong. Strong application controls are necessary, but insufficient if weak general controls exist. Subject to further investigation, it appears that the general controls over the database need to be strengthened.

Domain 3 – Answers to Practice Questions

1. **A** Time-sharing and leasing companies are not commonly primary sources of systems. These are normally required from dealers and distributors.
2. **C** While A, B, and D are all potential advantages in acquiring a computer package, the risk remains with the acquirer of the package.
3. **B** IS audit has a role in providing advice and assistance in control aspects of systems acquisition. Audit should not be involved in the implementation of controls while reduction in costs and tailoring of the package are management functions.
4. **A** User selection is not seen as part of the external acquisition process and the primary objective of external acquisition is to reduce the need for programming in-house.
5. **D** The RFI is intended to cover the functional definitions, access control constraints, and to acquire information on currently available products.
6. **D** The RFP is a Request for Proposal and is intended to elicit bids from vendors based on information provided regarding the functional requirements and access control constraints.
7. **A** The role of the user within requirements definition is to ensure the functional requirements for the proposed system are included within the definition accurately and completely. Access control constraints, implementations schedules, and support levels are technical requirements and fall within the remit of the IT function.
8. **D** System problem response times from the software supplier would typically be included in the proposal.

9. **D** The systems maintenance review covers both hardware and software and is conducted to ensure existing systems are operating as intended.

10. **A** The feasibility study, as its name suggests, is an evaluation of the likelihood of a successful implementation of the new system, or changes to the system. Programming language, documentation, and number of sites would not normally form part of the feasibility study.

11. **C** Bridges into existing systems are typically required where the degree of integration is low. Highly integrated systems, or where significant parts of old systems will be retained, reduce the need for bridges, and if no integration is required, no bridges are required.

12. **D** In conducting a feasibility study, no bias should pertain towards in-house, purchased, or externally developed systems. Any form of bias will distort the validity of the feasibility study.

13. **D** Development methodology and the availability of resources as well as a detailed system specification would not normally form part of a feasibility study. These would come at the detailed specification stage. Access controls, on the other hand, would be considered in terms of feasibility although not necessarily designed in detail.

14. **D** The outcome of a feasibility study could be any of the above based on information obtained during the study itself.

15. **A** Business disruptions commonly come about because of the need to retrain existing user staff who are continuing to operate existing systems.

16. **B** A common source of new system failure is a failure to ensure that valid data has been converted accurately and completely. Programs may be needed to convert the data or the data may be reloaded from scratch depending on the data needs of the new system and the quality of data retained within the existing system.

17. **B** System maintenance does not form a stage and system development of systems design, development, and utilization are all major control stages.

18. **D** Transaction processing systems, management information systems, and decision support systems are all types of system models.
19. **D** The value of knowledge to the organization is the fundamental on which information resource management rests.
20. **D** COBIT® defines accuracy, completeness, and usefulness as general control objectives for information processing.
21. **A** Transaction recording control objectives cover the input of transactions.
22. **A** Programmed balancing is a control technique to ensure input has been captured accurately and completely.
23. **A** Document scanning assists in ensuring that data capture errors are minimized and that input has been accurately captured.
24. **B** Programmed balancing is typically incorporated into an application program to ensure the accuracy and completeness of file update and report processing.
25. **C** User involvement is a common control over outputs to ensure the satisfy user needs from a business perspective.

5

DOMAIN 4 – INFORMATION SYSTEMS OPERATIONS, MAINTENANCE, AND SERVICE MANAGEMENT

This chapter covers the management of information systems operations, maintenance, and services.

This domain approximates 20% of the examination, that is some 30 questions. Ten tasks and 23 knowledge statements are included within this domain.

The IT auditor is required to evaluate the overall IT service management framework and practices within the organization in order to determine whether the controls and service levels achieve the objectives laid down by management and whether strategic objectives are met. This involves the auditor conducting periodic reviews of information systems in order to determine whether, on an ongoing basis, they continue to meet the organization's objectives. Operations of the IT function must be reviewed in order to evaluate whether they are controlled effectively and continue to support the organization's objectives. This includes the management of IT maintenance in terms of system upgrades as well as the day-to-day scheduling of jobs and the management of performance.

It is common for this function to handle the management of database integrity as well as ensuring the optimization of database configurations and the quality of data, and this would form a critical part of IT audit within this area.

This is the operational area where unforeseen problems are most likely to occur with such incidents requiring timely and effective responses and the auditor must examine the policies and procedures in place to ensure the detection, analysis, and resolution of the incidents.

Service level expectations are generally derived from the organization's business objectives. IT service delivery includes IS operations and IT services, as well as management of IS and the groups responsible for supporting them. IT services are built on service management frameworks covering all Processing Components, including:

Hardware

Hardware consists of those components which can physically be touched and manipulated.

Principal among those components are:

CPU

The Central Processing Unit is the heart of the computer. This is the logic unit which handles the arithmetic processing of all calculations.

Peripherals

Peripheral devices are those devices that attach to the CPU to handle, typically inputs and outputs. These include:

Terminals
Printers
Disk and tape devices

Memory

Memory takes the form in modern computers of silicon chips capable of storing information. In commercial computers, this information takes the form of 1 and 0 in the notation known as *binary*. Memory comes in various forms including:

RAM. Random Access Memory whose contents can be changed but which is vulnerable to loss of power where the contents of memory may also be lost. This type of memory is also known as *dynamic* or *volatile* memory.

ROM. Read-Only Memory is a form of memory whereby instructions are 'burned-in' and not lost in the event of a power loss. These programs cannot generally be changed. This is also known as non-volatile memory.

PROM. Programmable Read-Only Memory is similar to ROM but can have the contents changed.

EPROM. Erasable Programmable Read-Only Memory is similar to PROM, but the instructions can be erased by ultraviolet light.

There is another version of memory known as *non-volatile RAM*. This is memory which has been attached to a battery so that, in the event of a power loss, the contents will not be lost.

Computer Types

Mainframe computers. Large (physically as well as in power) computers used by companies to carry out large volume processing and concentrated computing:

Minicomputers. Physically smaller than mainframes although the power of many minicomputers and super-minis exceeds that of recent mainframes.

Microcomputers. Physically small computers with limited processing power and storage. Having said that, the power and capacity of today's micro is equivalent to that of a mainframe only 2–3 years ago.

Thin client. Personal computers that are commonly configured with minimal hardware features (e.g. diskless workstation). Most processing occurs at the server level using software, such as Microsoft Terminal Services or Citrix Presentation Server, to access a suite of applications.

Mobile Devices. These include handheld devices which may function as a small computing device as a substitute for a laptop computer. Such devices commonly combine telephone/email, computing, and wireless features together so they can be used anytime and anywhere.

Networks

LANs. Local Area Networks are collections of computers linked together within a comparatively small area.

WANs. Wide Area Networks are collections of computers spread over a large geographical area.

Proxy servers. These provide an intermediate link between users and resources. Proxy servers access services on a user's behalf. A proxy server may be used to provide a more secure and faster response than direct access utilizing inbuilt features such as firewalls and encryption.

Storage

Data are stored in a variety of forms for both permanent and temporary retention.

Bits. Binary digits, individual ones and zeros.

Bytes. Collections of bits making up individual characters. One byte is made up of 8 bits.

Disks. Large capacity storage devices containing anything from 10 Gb to 150 Tb of data. Note sizes are generally graded in *Kb (Kilobytes), Mb (Megabytes), Gb (Gigabytes), Tb (Terabytes), Pb (Petabytes)*. Each grade is 1000 times bigger than the previous.

Optical Disks. Laser encoded disks containing between 650 Mb and 10 Tb of data.

Thumb Drives (USB Flash Drives, Memory Card). These are removable memory devices with an integrated USB interface and range in capacity from 4 Mb to 2 Tb.

USB (Universal Serial Bus). A common connectivity interface designed to facilitate the connection of a variety of peripherals via a single standardized socket such that devices may be hot-swapped without the need to reboot the computer. In general, USB ports have replaced seal, parallel, and in some cases VGA and sound connectivity with significant improvements in terms of both speed and number of connections possible. Due to the ease of connectivity and extreme portability of peripherals such as Thumb Drives, USB ports must be viewed as risk areas for data theft, loss of confidentiality, introduction of viruses, and data corruption.

Tapes. Reel-to-reel or cassette.

Memory. As above.

Communications

In order to maximize the potential of the effective use of the information on computers it is essential that isolated computers be able to communicate and share data, programs. and hardware devices.

Terminals. Remote devices allowing the input and output to and from the computer of data and programs.

Modem. MOdulator/DEModulator, which translates digital computer signals into analog signals for telephone wires and retranslates them at the other end.

Multiplexer. Combining signals from a variety of devices to maximize utilization of expensive communication lines.

Cable. Metallic cable, usually copper, which can carry the signal between computers. These may come in the form of 'twisted pair' where two or more cables are strung together within a plastic sleeve, or in co-axial form where cables run within a metallic braiding in the same manner as a television aerial cable.

Fiber Optics. These consist of fine strands of fiberglass or plastic filaments which carry light signals without the need for electrical insulation. They have extremely high capacity and transfer rates but are expensive.

Microwave. This form of communication involves sending high-power signals from a transmitter to a receiver. They work on a direct line-of-sight basis but require no cabling.

Input

Inputs to computer systems have developed rapidly over the years. The IS auditor will still occasionally encounter some of the earlier types.

Cards. Rarely seen nowadays, punched cards were among the first input and output media and consisted of cardboard sheets, some eight inches by four inches with 80 columns where rectangular holes could be punched in combinations to represent numeric, alphabetic, and special characters.

Paper Tape. Another early input/output medium, paper tape was a low-cost alternative to punched cards and consisted of one-inch-wide paper tape with circular holes punched to form the same range of characters.

Keyboards. Still the most common input device today (although that is changing). Most keyboards are still based upon the original typist's qwerty keyboard design.

Mouse. An electromechanical pointing device used for inputting instructions in real time.

Scanners. Optical devices which can scan images into a digitized computer-readable form. These devices may be used in combination with Optical Character Recognition (OCR) software to allow the computer to interpret the pictures of data into actual characters.

Bar Codes and QR scanners. Optically recognizable printing which can be interpreted by low-cost scanners, these were originally designed for the automotive industry in Japan but are common in retail operations.

Voice Recognition. Perhaps the future of computer input whereby the computer user, programmer. or auditor simply dictates into a microphone and the computer responds appropriately.

Output

As with inputs, outputs are changing rapidly. In the earliest of computing times, output came in three basic forms. The most common of these was paper, however, quantities of cards and paper tape were output for subsequent re-processing. Nowadays most outputs are via screens or directly onto magnetic media.

Paper. Still a popular output medium, paper may be in continuous stationary form, cut sheet form, pre-printed business stock such as invoices, or negotiable instruments such as checks.

Computer. Output directly to another computer common in the age of the Internet and Cloud computing.

Screen. Output to screen is the current norm for the majority of outputs with graphics, tables, and charts and three-dimensional forms possible.

Microfilm/fiche. For permanent, readable recording of outputs with a small storage space required, microfilm is a popular output medium. Each frame contains one page of printed output. An alternative is the creation of microfiche measuring approximately 6 inches by 4 inches and containing some 200 pages of printout.

Magnetic Media. Output to disks, diskettes, and tapes is commonly used to store large volumes of information.

Voice. Another new output medium is voice where a permanent record is not required.

Control

Within the computer systems, control is exercised at a variety of points within the overall architecture. At each stage, opportunities exist to vary the manner in which the computer systems perform to meet the needs of the users.

Operating System. The Operating System is the set of programs which controls the basic operations of the computer. All other software runs under the direction of the Operating System and relies upon its services for all of the work they undertake.

Systems Software

Systems software includes computer programs and routines controlling computer hardware, processing, and non-user functions. This category includes the Operating Systems, telecommunications software, and data management software.

Auditing Operating Systems

In truth, it is unlikely that the auditor will ever actually audit the Operating System itself. Rather, the auditor will examine the operating environment and the way in which it has been implemented and controlled.

With no computer assistance available, the auditor can still look for normal controls such as segregation of duties, authorization of work etc. It is still possible to seek abnormalities such as excessive machine usage, regular late hours, and the like. A more effective audit will involve using the computer to audit the computer. This will typically involve the use of CAATs such as generalized audit software, specialized audit software, or utilities.

Prior to the use of such CAATs it is essential that the auditor knows what he or she wants to do. General browsing is expensive, does not inspire confidence and, worst of all, it usually does not work. A manual audit and auditor should know what they want to look at, where to find it, how to get it, and what they will do with it.

The auditor should always bear in mind the axiom that, to be wise, never believe what the first printout tells you. Ultimately, the auditor is not there to exercise control, the manager is, and the auditor should check the controls the manager relies on.

Utility Programs. This software, commonly supplied with the hardware or systems software, is designed to perform common and repetitive tasks such as sorting files, printing, copying, and comparing files.

As such these can be powerful tools for the auditor to employ. There are two main types of utility software. The first type is used in the system development process to improve productivity, such as program development aids and online editors. The second type is used to assist in the management of the operation of the computer system, such as performance monitors, job schedulers, and disk management systems. Utility software may have privileged access capabilities at all times, some of the time, or never. Privileged access allows programs or users to perform functions that may bypass normal security.

Application Systems. These systems perform the business functions required of the computer. They run under the direct control of the Operating System but may contain many powerful control elements themselves.

Parameters. These are user-defined variations adjusting the manner in which programs normally operate.

Run Instructions. These are instructions to operators of computers instructing them on the jobs to be run and responses to machine questions to be entered.

JCL. Job Control Language is a means of automating the job running process by giving the computer the instructions in a form of batch programming language.

The Human Element. Ultimately control is exercised by the people who use, operate, program, and manage computers.

People

Operators. These run the computers on a day-to-day basis.

Programmers. They write the application programs which run on the computer.

Systems Designers. They design the overall structure of the application systems and specify the programs required.

Systems Analysts. They analyze the business structures, applications, and procedures to determine what, if any, contribution IS can make. They will also design the outline business specifications of new systems.

Systems Programmers. Responsible for the well-being of the Operating Systems and the related systems software components.

Database Analysts. Responsible for maintaining the Database Management System (DBMS) which is the systems software component controlling access to and format of the data.

Network Analysts. Responsible for ensuring availability, performance standards, and security are achieved on networks.

Management. Plan, organize, and direct to ensure corporate objectives are achieved.

Data typically consists of:

- Fields held in:
- Records or Tuples (in a relational database) held in:
- Files or Tables (in a relational database) held on:
- Disk.

Change control and end-user-computing also fall under this domain, as does continuity and resilience management including the IT disaster recovery plan.

Generically IT service management (ITSM) refers to all the activities, policies, and processes that organizations use for deploying, managing, and improving IT service delivery and focuses on aligning

IT services with the needs of business through a variety of detailed practices.

Job Scheduling

A job schedule is used in complex environments to automate processing by listing the jobs to be run and the order in which they are to be run. In days gone by this was a manual process but in today's complex environment automated job scheduling software is used to facilitate the processing of batch runs as well as maintenance activities such as backups. Scheduling software may also be used to optimize resource utilization by allocating resources to higher priority jobs.

System Interfaces

Frameworks

Common Frameworks include COBIT® from ISACA, ITIL, and the Microsoft Operations Framework among many others. From a CISA perspective, COBIT® forms the principal framework for examination.

As previously stated, *Control Objectives for Information and related Technology* (COBIT®) is one of the most widely accepted models of IT governance and control utilized to manage risks and implement controls within an IT environment in order to achieve business objectives. COBIT® was introduced to meld existing IT standards and best practices into one comprehensive structure designed to achieve international accepted governance standards. Working from the strategic requirements of the organization, COBIT® encompasses the full range of IT activities focusing on the achievement of control objectives rather than the implementation of specific controls. As such, it integrates and aligns IT practices with organizational governance and strategic requirements. It is not the only set of standards in common use, but it integrates with other standards to achieve defined levels of control.

As stated by ISACA,

COBIT® 5 is the latest edition of ISACA's globally accepted framework, providing an end-to-end business view of the governance of enterprise IT that reflects the central role of information and technology in creating value for enterprises. The principles, practices, analytical tools and models found in COBIT® 5 embody thought leadership and guidance from business, IT and governance experts around the world.[*]

What may be classed as best practice for an organization must be appropriate to that organization based upon its needs and capabilities. Standards themselves do not achieve best practice but require careful selection, interpretation, and implementation in order to achieve an adequacy of control. At its highest level, COBIT® presents a framework for overall control based upon a model of IT processes intended as a generic model upon which specific controls can be overlaid in order to achieve a unique system of internal controls specifically tailored to the business needs of the organization. COBIT® is designed to be utilized at different levels of management.

Executive management can utilize it to ensure value is obtained from the significant investment in IT and to ensure that risk and control investment is appropriately balanced. From an operational management perspective, COBIT® facilitates the gaining of assurance that the management and control of IT services, whether insourced or outsourced, is appropriate. IT management can use it as an operational tool to ensure the business strategy is supported in a controlled and appropriately managed manner in providing IT services. IT auditors can utilize COBIT® to evaluate the adequacy of controls, design appropriate tests to determine the effectiveness of controls, and provide management with appropriate advice on the system of internal controls.

COBIT® utilizes a framework of domains and processes in order to create a logical structure of IT activities in a manner that can be easily subject to managerial controls.

The COBIT® 5 framework is built on five basic principles, which are covered in detail, and includes extensive guidance on enablers for governance and management of enterprise IT. These include:

- Meeting stakeholder needs
- Covering the enterprise end-to-end
- Applying a single integrated framework
- Enabling a holistic approach

---

[*] http://www.isaca.org/COBIT®/Pages/COBIT®-5-Framework-product-page.aspx

- Separating Governance from Management

ITIL

IT Infrastructure Library (ITIL) (www.itil.org) is intended to define the best practice in IT Service Management. It was developed by the Office of Government Commerce (OGC) and is supported by publications, qualifications, and an international user group. The approach is a top-down, business-driven approach to the management of IT, which is intended to address the need to deliver a high-quality IT service in order to deliver strategic business value. IT Service Management focuses on the people, processes, and technology issues that IT organizations face. ITIL, itself, attempts to assist organizations to develop a framework for IT Service Management by providing a cohesive set of best practices, drawn from both the public and private sectors. It offers a comprehensive qualifications scheme and accredited training organizations, as well as specifically developed implementation and assessment tools.

There are five ITIL books covering:

- **Service Strategy:** This book provides a view of ITIL that aligns business and information technology.
- **Service Design:** This book provides guidance upon the production/maintenance of information technology policies, architectures, and documents.
- **Service Transition:** The book focuses on the change management role and release practices, for the transition of services into any business environment.
- **Service Operation:** This book focuses on delivery and control process activities and is based on a selection of service support and service delivery control points.
- **Continual Service Improvement:** In this book, the process elements involved in identifying and introducing service management improvements, as well as issues surrounding service retirement, are examined in detail.

ITIL V2 focusses specifically on the areas of Service Support and Service Delivery, with the former covering:

- Change Management
- Release Management
- Problem Management
- Incident Management
- Configuration Management

while Service Delivery includes:

- IT Financial Management
- IT Continuity Management
- Capacity Management
- Availability Management
- Service Level Management
- Service Desk

Change Management

Periodically the necessity arises to modify an existing hardware and/or software configuration as a result of:

- Hardware changes as a result of performance improvements or reconfigurations caused by changes to other systems
- Hardware failures during normal operations
- The detection of a software error during normal operations
- Changes to legislation affecting the organization's business systems
- A change to the business operation of the organization requiring alterations within the information systems

As a result of these changes in the environment, the extent of change required within the existing system configuration must be determined and the change applied in a controlled manner so as to avoid any undue disruption to normal processing. It is critical that during periods of change, the production versions of software are protected against unauthorized changes, untested changes, or even malicious changes.

This control requires a coordinated effort involving managers, users, information systems personnel, and IT auditors. An effective methodology for authorizing, testing, and implementing the change in a controlled manner is a prerequisite. In most organizations this will involve the use of a *Change Control Committee* involving members of all of the aforementioned disciplines. This committee is normally involved in evaluating change requests for corporate or control implications, authorization of those requests, ensuring that testing and documentation of the changes have been carried out, and finally, authorizing the implementation of the change into the live environment.

All requests for amendments to production programs should be made in writing and include the business justification for the change requested. A full appraisal of the impacts, justification, and alternatives considered should be undertaken with more significant changes being subject to more stringent checks. If the change is of a major nature, a feasibility study may be required.

Once changes are approved by the committee, the work may be undertaken by such resources as the committee approves (normally IT with some user involvement) and, once the programmer involved is satisfied that the amended software is working as intended, independent testing should take place with the user participation prior to implementation in the production environment. Users, IT staff, and auditors should all sign off on the change to ensure that their individual needs have been satisfied. It should be stressed that when the IT auditor signs off on a change, this is an indication that the audit's control requirements have been met within the change system. It is not an indication of quality assurance of the system because this is the responsibility of both the users and IT management.

All changes to systems, whether hardware, software, or both, should be fully documented with the effects of all maintenance changes so that subsequent work on the relative systems can be expedited. With all possible care being taken there is still a chance that a change to a system will result in a production system failure. As such, operations recoverability procedures should be in place in the event of a system failure in the new configuration. This would typically involve securing the condition of the system and data prior to the change being implemented so that an unsuccessful change can be appropriately reversed.

Within a mainframe environment it is common to separate the production and development versions of programs using completely segregated software libraries. Once implementation has been authorized, the change controller will normally copy the amended source code into the production library. For this to be effective, access to production libraries must be restricted to the change controller only. This access control is intended to prevent both accidental and malicious amendments to production software occurring without appropriate authorization.

Updating software on personal computers, mobile devices, and local area networks would appear more straightforward because they normally involve installation of purchased packages. Unfortunately, not all purchased packages function immediately as intended. In the smaller environment of personal computers, it is common that backups are not taken prior to system changes and that the introduction of a new version of software or even new software altogether may result in significant damage to the production environment.

Change Management in the Use of Cloud-Based Applications

Cloud computing is now a significant IT innovation and impacts the organization's business model, impacting IT roles, service delivery, and processes. Cloud computing changes the way an IT team works and the kinds of jobs they do. The extent of such changes mainly depends on the nature of cloud servicing in use (e.g. SaaS, PaaS, IaaS) as well as the chosen deployment models (e.g. Private, Public, Hybrid, Community).

Where the device uses Cloud-based technology, the traditional Change Management process in the Cloud has the following additional challenges:

- Need to validate change request and approval.
- Identifying the right balance for approving Cloud-based changes.

These are conventionally addressed in a variety of ways. Cloud-based tools are available which can undertake configuration changes and track management approval process and can be adapted to approve or decline additional configuration or subscription changes.

Standard change requests (pre-approved) which follow pre-defined rules, parameters, and cost-limits, can be automated, allowing Cloud customers the benefits derivable from the scalability and elasticity of service offered by the Cloud in a controlled and pre-defined manner.

Generally, public Cloud providers have available a variety of tools that are used for Configuration and Change Management in the Cloud. Such tools are used to capture information such as cloud resources currently being utilized, changes in resource usage changes, and the like.

Problem Management

The changes thus controlled (in-house or Cloud) are known and planned changes. The procedures involve ensuring prior authorization for all changes, supervision of the change process, adequate testing of all changes, and user sign-off on all changes. Periodically things will go wrong with a system, which necessitates an urgent repair. Such changes are not known in advance and are commonly executed, and permission sought retrospectively. Such changes are controlled using *Problem Management*. Problem Management's objective is to control systems during emergency situations arising from unforeseen changes. Typically, this will involve bypassing of normal control mechanisms and may require direct programmer access to live data. This must be controlled separately and must involve user authorization, even retrospectively.

Auditing Change Control

From an audit perspective, the IT auditor will seek assurance that change control procedures are in place and effective over changes to hardware, software, telecommunications, or anything that affects the processing environment. Sources of evidence for the auditor would include minutes of change control committee meetings, software movement reports, access control logs, and system failure records.

Service Management

Service management involves the provision and operation of services to the organization by IT. Defining and delivering Services (value, outcome, risk, and resource optimization) to the business or to customers is the ultimate mission of any IT organization. By creating a formal framework for measuring current service improvement projects, it is possible to benchmark against best practices across the industry. This is intended to lead to competitive gains through the promotion of cost-effective services delivered in a consistent manner. In achieving this, IT can undergo a paradigm shift from reactive processing to proactively driving.

In CISA terms, IT is today being measured based on service performance, including performance measures for setting up new or changed services via projects. Services are being organized by defined and accepted processes, functions (organizations, people, and technology) – all those are leveraged resources or, in COBIT® terms, *enablers*. Services, processes, organization, people, and technology are being managed by a set of control objectives. These are frequently structured into an 'IT balanced scorecard'. Under COBIT® 5 the balanced scorecard (BSC) methodology for structuring and communicating performance measurement places it more prominently at the front of the framework in the goals cascade. This is based upon the work done by David Norton and Robert Kaplan in the mid-1990s. It involves expanding the drivers to include the evaluation of service delivery from the *Customer Perspective*, the *Internal Business Processes*, and the *Learning and Growth* perspectives as well as the conventional *Financial Perspective*.

Disaster Recovery Planning

The Operations area of IT is typically responsible to ensure business continuity in the event of a computer disaster. Perhaps the best-prepared organizations are the ones who have lived through a calamity.

Among the IT risks faced by an organization are:

- Fire
- Flood
- Building collapse
- Explosion
- Industrial failure
- Power failure
- Loss of data
- Deliberate sabotage
- Computer abuse

- Deliberate action by staff
- 'Hacking' into systems
- Internet penetration
- EDI abuse

As can be seen, many of these risks have nothing to do with computer systems but remain for the enterprise as a whole. There is a tendency to focus upon the Information Systems to the exclusion of all else within the organization, and this is as dangerous as not looking at contingency planning at all.

In all these cases a different approach to recovery planning is required. The plan for evacuation of the building to a new location is inappropriate if the disaster involves the loss of a small but vital file.

As such an IT Disaster Recovery Plan must be capable of responding to a variety of 'Disasters' and provide optimal solutions for each.

In all these cases a different approach to recovery planning is required. The plan for evacuation of the building to a new location is inappropriate if the disaster involves the loss of a small but vital file.

As such a Disaster Recovery Plan (DRP) must be capable of responding to a variety of 'Disasters' and provide optimal solutions for each.

As with any other form of business analysis, the beginning involves understanding the business. In DRP terms this means modeling the business, identifying data flow, and dependencies and identifying the critical systems as well as any dependent systems (including manual systems).

Data used within each system needs to be graded by application and therefore by strategic importance as well as by alternate methods of sourcing and degree of pain in loss. In a comprehensive plan data may even be rated by disruption period.

Auditing the DRP involves investigating and evaluating the policies, application systems covered, user data defined, hardware required, systems software needed, and the realism of the testing. Overall, the auditor must evaluate the probability of business continuity.

The auditor must also be satisfied that the plan itself will be kept up-to-date and appropriate. This means that the auditor must:

- Ensure responsibility for plan maintenance
- Ensure management is kept informed

- Ensure the master copy of the plan is secure
- Ensure distributed copies are kept up-to-date and secure

Auditing Service Delivery

From an audit perspective, IT service delivery can be seen as an operational audit within the areas of configuration and change management, capacity management, service level agreement management, business continuity management, and incident management. In each of these areas the auditor must clearly understand the objectives sought by the organization and the measurement criteria applied by management in order to judge the accomplishment of those objectives on an ongoing basis, including:

- **Configuration and Change Management**

    Configuration management involves the maintaining of a detailed inventory of the resources within the organization used in the provision of IT services. This goes beyond the traditional asset register since it must address hardware, software, networking, and knowledge. It must also include information regarding the existence, location, state of maintenance, problems encountered, and resolution action taken for each of the resources. The IT auditor must evaluate the process by which configuration management is carried out in order to achieve a corporate objective.

    In the absence of an effective change management process, an 'insignificant' change in an operating environment such as the implementation of a new service pack can cause disruption or even failure within a critical operational area. Change management ensures that all changes to all critical resources are implemented in a planned and authorized manner.

    The auditor must ensure that, in addition to ensuring appropriate authorization of such changes, appropriate planning, testing, and implementation and, in case of a change failure, the development of a fallback plan takes place.

- **Capacity Management**

    Every individual resource contributing towards the provision of IT services will be of limited capacity. This includes human resources as well as technical resources. Effective Information Systems assisting in the growth of the business inevitably increase the workload on all resources. Effective service management requires effective capacity management wherein the capacity of each individual component is known, monitored, and the load balanced in order to achieve optimal performance.

Once again, the auditor will seek to determine that appropriate process exists to monitor resource utilization and to plan for the increasing capacity inevitably required.

- **Service Level Agreement Management**

   Service level agreements (SLA) are written commitments that the IT function will deliver a level of service acceptable to the user and are normally defined in terms of response time, uptime, hardware and software error rates, and problem resolution time. It is common for IT to utilize software solutions to record incidents and the resolution, and the auditor must determine whether SLAs exist, are adequately monitored, provided meaningful management information, and are used by management to improve service delivery.

- **Business Continuity Management**

   This area is fully discussed in Chapter 3 in this book. The auditor would typically seek to determine that business continuity management is carried out, has been assigned to a knowledgeable person with appropriate authorities, is tested regularly, and works.

- **Incident Management**

   Incident management involves the recording of all incidents as they happen, including the quantification of the impact on the business (users impacted, customers affected, impact on corporate image, impact on revenues, and cash flow). In addition, the process also seeks to determine the actual cause and appropriate resolution of the problem.

   The auditor must determine that an appropriate and effective incident management process has been implemented within the organization and is monitored appropriately by management.

The *financial* aspects of service center management involve the acquisition of the whole infrastructure and the most cost-effective price to the organization. This does not necessarily mean that the price of acquisition will always be the lowest because the aforementioned aspects such as reliability and availability must be taken into consideration. Only when costs are fully known and attributable to individual business functionality can cost benefit be truly and accurately identified.

The IT auditor needs to be familiar with the many terms encountered in costing service center management. Most important of these is the distinction among:

- *Direct costs*, which are related to the specific item or function and can be attributed to it in a feasible way.
- *Indirect costs*, which are related to the specific item or function but cannot be attributed to it in a feasible way. Indirect costs are then allocated or assigned using an appropriate cost allocation method.
- *Variable costs*, which change in direct proportion to the volume of outputs.
- *Fixed costs*, which do not vary with volumes produced, but are fixed, for example, equipment rentals payable irrespective of usage.

Different costing approaches are used by different organizations with varying implications. These are typically determined not only by the specific business processes or services provided, but also by the types of costing systems generally in use in the sector that the organization is engaged in, such as manufacturing, service, or merchandising sectors.

An IT auditor may become involved in operational audits of the service center to determine the reasonableness of costs attributable to individual user areas. Disagreements commonly arise regarding the assignment of fixed and variable overhead costs to individual users of services, particularly in a mainframe environment where the majority of hardware costs cannot be related to individual users using direct costing. In such environments, system usage is a commonly used alternative.

Such allocations of cost may directly affect the remuneration of user managers who may seek to have a look at costs transferred to other users in order to defend bonuses or departmental profitability.

One final area of cost within a service center is the overall *cost of quality*, which can impact both performance evaluation and customer satisfaction. Specific costs within these areas include *prevention costs* to ensure delivery at the service level specified, *appraisal costs* incurred in monitoring service delivery, *internal failure costs* where costs are incurred as a result of failures within the service center itself, they reach the user and where a service has to be re-performed.

Overall, *Service Level Management* involves ensuring that the services requested and agreed on with functional user management are delivered on an ongoing basis as and how they have been committed to be delivered. Achieving service level management is dependent upon the achievement of all the other areas of service delivery previously mentioned, thus providing a framework upon which an effective and efficient range of services can be delivered in a secure manner.

This management is normally measured against the *Service Level Agreement*.

Domain 4 – Practice Questions

1. The technical infrastructure includes everything below *except*:
   a. Routers.
   b. Application software.
   c. Operating system utilities.
   d. Networks.

2. Effective configuration management requires:
   a. Identification, control, status, and verification.
   b. Identification, status, implementation, and verification.
   c. Identification, control, maintenance, and implementation.
   d. Control, implementation, status, and verification.

3. A clear architecture covering the technical infrastructure assists systems development by:
   a. Enforcing standardization.
   b. Minimizing systems destruction in the event of a failure.
   c. Maintaining an asset register.
   d. Permitting the modularization of application systems.

4. An IS auditor has discovered a weakness in access controls to program and data files. However, management feels that its daily review of activity audit trails provides a compensating control. Which of the following would be LEAST important in evaluating the adequacy of this control?
   a. The type of information written to the audit trail file.
   b. How well the audit trails file is protected.
   c. The identity of the person authorized to change what is written to the audit trail file.
   d. The retention period of the audit trail file.

5. Continuous auditing on a high volume, transaction-based system in real-time may be:
   a. Implemented at minimal cost.
   b. Implemented using generalized audit software.
   c. Detrimental to normal business processing.
   d. Implemented manually.

6. Operations exposures include:
   a. Predefined run schedules.
   b. Systems performance statistics.
   c. Human error.
   d. Adequate supervision.

7. Which of the following pairs of job functions/duties would an organization MOST likely keep separate?
   a. Operations and programming.
   b. Systems analyst and applications programmer.
   c. Database administrator and IS manager.
   d. Tape librarian and program librarian.

8. In an organization where a complete separation of duties cannot be achieved in an online system, which of the following transaction functions should NOT be performed by the operations personnel?
   a. Origination.
   b. Authorization.
   c. Recording.
   d. All of the above.

9. Continuity management within a service center can be seen as:
   a. A technical problem.
   b. Responsibility of IT.
   c. A business problem with a technical solution.
   d. Too critical a component to rely on reactive measures.

10. In the event of a computer disaster without an effective contingency plan being in place, the likelihood of business collapse is primarily dependent upon:
    a. Criticality of IT services provided.
    b. Size of the organization.
    c. Experience of service center management.
    d. Whether a hot site is available.

11. The purpose of a Business Impact Analysis is to:
    a. Identify the critical information systems.
    b. Identify which systems to recover first.
    c. Identify the critical processes within the organization and support structures provided by information systems.
    d. Identify the components used in supporting critical systems.

12. Capacity planning involves:
    a. Ensuring information processing resources have sufficient capacity to handle peak loads.
    b. Ensuring information processing resources have sufficient capacity to handle agreed loads.
    c. Ensuring information processing resources have sufficient capacity to handle average loads.
    d. Ensuring information processing resources have sufficient capacity to handle minimum loads.

13. Ensuring systems availability includes evaluating:
    a. Effectiveness of the disaster recovery plan.
    b. The existence of the disaster recovery plan.
    c. The resilience of the system.
    d. The capacity of the system.

14. A cost which is related to specific function that cannot be attributed to it in a feasible way is:
    a. An indirect cost.
    b. A direct cost.
    c. A fixed cost.
    d. A variable cost.

15. Prevention cost is part of:
    a. Direct costs.
    b. Fixed costs.
    c. Variable costs.
    d. Cost of quality.

16. In a service center context, a service level agreement may be a contract between:
    a. IT and its user areas.
    b. IT audit and IT user areas.
    c. Hardware and software suppliers and IT.
    d. All of the above.

17. Effective supplier management is based on:
    a. SLAs with contract penalties.
    b. Clearly defined requirements in the RFP.
    c. Measurable service levels and regular monitoring.
    d. Strong negotiation skills of the procurement team.

Domain 4 – Review Questions and Hands-On Exercise

- Describe the effects of the integration of Hardware, Software, and Networks.
- Explain the need for IT control monitoring and evaluation tools, such as access control systems monitoring.
- Explain the management of information resources and information infrastructure and discuss the use of enterprise management software.
- Describe the service center management and operations standards/guidelines contained within COBIT®, ITIL, and ISO17799.

- Discuss the issues and considerations of service center vs. proprietary technical infrastructures.
- Describe the role and tasks of the operations department and discuss the risks inherent in such an environment together with the control opportunities.
- Explain how such operations departments can be audited.
- Describe service center management and operations in terms of standards and guidelines.
- Explain how change management/implementation of new and changed systems occurs including the organization of the tools used to control the introduction of new and changed products into the service center environment including the administration of release and versions of automated systems.
- Explain how security management relates to resource/configuration management via compliance with organization/IT operating standards, policies and procedures, problem, and incident management.
- Describe IS management's role in capacity planning and prognosis.
- Describe the issues in management of the distribution of automated systems.
- Explain management's relation with suppliers and customer liaison utilizing service level management.
- Describe the steps required to establish the risk profile of the organization.
- Define the factors affecting the quality of the Business Impact Analysis.
- Describe a methodology in order to identify those systems and key personnel which are crucial to the ongoing survival of the organization.
- Describe the attributes of a cohesive and comprehensive plan.
- Describe the testing procedures for the contingency plan (CP).
- Define the extent of management support and commitment to the process.
- Describe how to evaluate the testing, maintenance, and revision of the plan.

Exercise 4

An IT division of a mid-sized bank has an off-site backup storage unit containing 5000 tape backups. Some are encrypted while others remain in cleartext. Transaction files are transferred electronically to the contracted hotsite which also has tape reading capability. Failover is tested regularly but management is concerned that, in an emergency requiring the use of the tapes, the data required will be missing, corrupt, or unusable. They have asked IT audit to assist in testing the backup and recovery procedures.

What manner of risks would the organization face and how would the auditor test the controls intended to mitigate the threats?

Exercise 4 Sample Answer

The major business risk is that the IT recovery is not achieved, and that the non-availability of the IT processing capability leads to a catastrophic loss of customer confidence such that the bank will be forced out of business. This could result from a number of potential control failures such as:

- Hotsite data and software not in sync with the main system.
- Hardware at the hotsite not compatible or out of date compared to the live site.
- Lack of bandwidth at the hotsite for the full operational load of the bank.
- Tape backups unreadable.
- Decryption drive out of sync with the originating drives or inoperative.
- Tapes missing, misplaced, or mislabeled.
- Tape backups are not complete sets for recovery.
- Full recovery from tapes inadequately tested or infrequently tested.
- Failover infrequently tested to systems recovered from tapes.

Auditor tests would involve:

- Assessing the adequacy of recovery plans.
- Evaluating the staff training of their place in the plan.
- Determining the nature, frequency, and success rate of testing.

- Checking the usability of a statistically valid sample of tapes.
- Interrogating tape usage log files for previous use in tests and currency of tapes.
- Observe an actual recovery test to determine adequacy and effectiveness of controls.
- Evaluate access rights for currency, authorization, and maintenance.

Domain 4 – Answers to Practice Questions

1. **B** Routers, networks, and operating system utilities all form part of the overall technical infrastructure under which application software runs.

2. **A** For configuration management to be effective, the state of implementation of all components is not essential.

3. **D** Application systems may be efficiently developed using modularization which is significantly assisted by having a clear architecture covering the technical infrastructure.

4. **D** The type of information written to the audit file combined with the audit trail protection including the identity of any person authorized to change the content of the audit trail file would be critical to evaluating the adequacy of the control. The retention period of the audit file, although essential, would be the least important of these.

5. **C** Any form of continuous auditing involves an overhead on automated processing. The higher the transaction volume, the greater the overhead, and therefore the more detrimental to normal business processing.

6. **C** Human error remains the most common operations exposure in Computer Systems. Predefined run schedules, performance statistics, and adequate supervision are all controls rather than exposures.

7. **A** Segregation of duties is critical in all of these functions, but operators should not be programming the machine and programmers should not be operating the machine.

8. **D** None of these transaction functions should be performed by operation personnel.

9. **D** Continuity management is intended to ensure continuity of processing in an emergency. As such, it may be seen as a critical component and too significant to rely on development only after an event occurs.

10. **A** When a computer disaster occurs, the likelihood of total business collapse depends on the criticality of the IT services provided and the impact of the unavailability for an extended period of time.

11. **C** The Business Impact Analysis is intended to identify the support structures provided by information systems to the most mission-critical business processes within the organization.

12. **B** Peak loads may occur rarely within the organization. These only form part of capacity planning when their likelihood of impact has been agreed in terms of the load to be handled. Neither the minimum load nor the average load would normally form part of capacity planning.

13. **C** The existence and capacity of the DRP as well as the capacity of the system all form part of the resilience of the system in terms of availability.

14. **A** Fixed costs, direct costs, and variable costs may all be attributed to a specific function in different ways. Indirect costs are, by their nature, unable to be attributed to a specific function.

15. **D** Prevention costs are those costs incurred in order to ensure ongoing quality of operations and outputs.

16. **D** Service level agreements are contracts which may involve all of the suppliers and users of IT services.

17. **A** Supplier management incorporates measurable service levels and clearly defined requirements, but ultimately are based on Service Level Agreements with contracted penalties for noncompliance.

6

DOMAIN 5 – PROTECTION OF INFORMATION ASSETS

This chapter covers the processes by which the organization's policies, standards, procedures, and controls ensure the confidentiality, integrity, and availability of information assets.

This domain has been defined by ISACA as the most critical of the CISA domains and approximates 25% of the examination, that is some 38 questions. Six tasks and 26 knowledge statements are included within this domain.

Within the CISA examination, candidates are examined to ensure their understanding of the security policies, standards, procedures, and controls established and implemented within the organization to achieve the confidentiality, integrity, and availability of information assets.

The tasks to be undertaken by the IT auditor may include:

- Evaluation of the corporate policies regarding information security and privacy as well as the standards and procedures in place to achieve completeness as well as the alignment with both generally accepted practices and compliance with any external requirements.
- Examination and evaluation of the design, implementation, maintenance, monitoring, and reporting of both physical and environmental controls in order to determine that the information assets are adequately safeguarded to meet corporate levels of requirement.
- Examination and evaluation of the design, implementation, maintenance, monitoring, and reporting all system and logical security controls designed to ensure the confidentiality, integrity, and availability of information.

- Examination and evaluation of the design, implementation, and monitoring of the processes by which data is classified as well as the procedures intended to ensure alignment with overall organizational policies, standards, and procedures as well as any applicable external requirements.
- The auditor is also required to evaluate the processes and procedures in place used to store, retrieve, transport, and dispose of assets in order to determine whether those information assets are adequately safeguarded.
- Evaluate the overall information security program in order to determine its effectiveness as well as its alignment in the overall organizational strategies and objectives.

The task statements define the areas within which the CISA candidate has adequate knowledge to carry out the functionality required. The specific areas where a good understanding is required in order to perform these tasks are spelled out in the knowledge statements covered in this chapter.

Protection of Information Assets

With today's integration of IT into business processes, threats to computerized assets are threats to business survival, effectiveness, and general quality. Combining both physical and logical controls, protection of information assets ensures a continuing availability of information systems as well as the integrity and confidentiality of the information stored on those systems. Advances in the legal systems surrounding information technology have made it more complicated to ensure conformity to all applicable laws, regulations, and standards on an international basis. The data are at the heart of the information assets and categorization forms a major part of the corporate classification of all information assets requiring definitions of:

- Ownership of the information asset
- Who has access rights and at what level
- The authority for determining the access rights and access privileges

- Granting of approvals
- Monitoring of access

Data integrity generally is taken to refer to the accuracy, completeness, validity, verifiability, and consistency of the data after it has been introduced into a system. Such integrity comes about as a result of the combination of effective internal controls and a knowledgeable user and management component.

Privacy Principles

Confidentiality of information must be treated on an organization-wide basis with privacy built into the policies, standards, and procedures governing the collection, use, disclosure, and destruction of sensitive information. All such sensitive information must be identified with the accountability for ensuring confidentiality clearly defined. This, then, forms the basis for informed decisions regarding systems policies, design, and operations with the overall objective of mitigating the inherent risks.

A common risk factor for confidentiality is the involvement of outside parties with data access, and the required levels of security control must be defined and agreed upon by the ability to monitor the controls implemented which must remain within the control of the organization. This would typically be laid out in the Service Level Agreement. At all events, data access must be granted on a need-to-have basis and minimized wherever possible.

Access by both third parties as well as employees should be subject to adequate screening, background verification, and ongoing monitoring both against the relevant laws and regulations as well as corporate ethical standards. This will typically involve an educational program to raise levels of awareness of information asset risk and security procedures. Formal disciplinary or contractual procedures will be required for handling any security breaches whether internal or external. Data Security must also be considered, e.g. exited employees, contractors, or third-party users including the removal of all access rights and the return of all equipment, access keys, identification cards, and any documentation identifying an individual as a current member of the organization.

Design, Implementation, Maintenance, Monitoring, and Reporting of Security Controls

Physical and Environmental Controls and Supporting Practices for the Protection of Information Assets

Environmental security encompasses the support structures that are the foundations of the physical environment including power, air conditioning, heating, and lighting.

In all cases, controls must be appropriate to the threats faced and therefore both physical and environmental controls become dictated by the overall risks and the environment.

- **Physical damage and destruction.** Physical damage may be of a temporary or permanent nature and require repair or replacement of equipment or of the system components affected. Damage could be minor such as physical damage to a data medium where and backup is available or could range to catastrophic such as damage to the whole installation and its personnel with little to no hope of immediate recovery. Such damage may also come as a result of malicious activities either from insiders or from individuals external to the organization. In either event, short or long-term disruption of information services may result. The duration of that interruption as well as the criticality of the service provided which could be interrupted will dictate the extent of potential losses to the organization and therefore the degree of control required for both short and long-term disruptions.

- **Loss of data confidentiality.** Where physical control over confidential outputs has been compromised, confidentiality may become degraded or lost totally resulting in information which may be classed as corporate critical or simply confidential ending up in the public domain. In many cases, such losses may be attributable to the easy availability of portable devices and storage mechanisms as well as the advent of cloud mechanisms for the detention of confidential data. Using access to the network in which the required information is stored, and these days that includes wireless networks, the replication and compromise of confidential information is relatively simple.

An area which is commonly overlooked when we examine vulnerable points of data confidentiality loss is the storage and security of backups. Even in systems where data confidentiality is achieved using extensive encryption, it may frequently be found that data backups are retained in an unencrypted form and are thus subject to potential unauthorized copying and disclosure. In addition, when problems are encountered in the use of computer equipment it is common practice to place the equipment in the hands of internal or external experts without consideration of the need to maintain confidentiality of any information on the faulty equipment resulting again in a potential of loss of confidentiality.

- **Theft of equipment.** One of the most commonly stolen electronic items these days is a smartphone which is, of course, simply a highly portable computer. The danger in such theft lies not only in the loss of equipment, but the access now available to the confidential information including communication passwords and the like stored in an unencrypted form on a portable device. While much corporate attention is paid to educate users about maintaining the security of mobile devices, it should be noted that even mainframes have been stolen in the past.

Physical Access Controls for the Identification,
Authentication, and Restriction of Users

Physical access controls are intended to manage the movements of personnel, media, and hardware and out of a controlled area as well as restricting access within that area. Controls will take a variety of forms including:

- Risk analysis of the computer environment in order to determine which areas will require higher levels of access so that such access may be granted again on a need-to-have basis.
- Adequate peripheral defenses over physical access in the form of walls or fences with restricted points of access. All access through these restricted points should include identification of undesirable items such as third-party hardware outside the

control of the organization, explosives, firearms, and the like. At this point, physical identification of acclaimed identity using card or biometric access systems as well as closed circuit television monitoring are typically used.

- In addition to the conventional key locks on doors, card locks, combination locks, and biometric blocks are all used in achieving physical security within the IT environment. Both key and card locks are themselves dependent on the physical security and restricted number of keys and cards issued. When used with turnstiles, access cards are also vulnerable to the cardholder entering then passing the card to a second person who also gains entry. Combination locks, while apparently more secure, are vulnerable to simple observation either by shoulder surfing (looking over the user's shoulder) or via closed circuit television cameras which have inadvertently, or otherwise, been directed at the combination lock.

  Biometric locks, such as those containing thumbprint scanners, provide a higher level of access authentication but even then, in common with all locked doors, suffer from the risk that one person will open the door and multiple people enter.

- Within the overall area being physically protected, there will typically be additional areas where higher levels of security will be required, and additional locks and authentication mechanisms have been implemented. It should, however, the remembered that in modern office areas many interior walls are built using prefabricated wall panels which can be moved around as required to fit the office environment. Such walls provide little protection against physical assault and in many cases lie beneath a suspended ceiling with a vault area providing physical access over the wall into the 'secure' area. The same logical flaw exists where raised floors are used in computer rooms and extend beyond the peripheral wall.

- Some computer installations are designed to operate unattended; motion detectors can be used to detect movement within a secure area as soon as periphery is breached.

- Disposal of outputs in a safe manner can maintain confidentiality and scrap leaves a secured area. Shredders of the appropriate type can make reassembly or shredded documents more difficult but, where microfilm or microfiche exist standard shredders may be inadequate, and incineration may be required.

- Disposal of outdated or obsolete equipment may carry within its components information which is confidential to the organization and, for example in the disposal of fixed disks and other storage media, destruction may be the safer option.
- When equipment repair is required, all sensitive media must be removed. If this is impossible, the security risk of handing over such equipment to a third party must be considered when the repair decision is made. It may be more cost-efficient in the long run to destroy the equipment rather than risk the loss of confidentiality.
- Removal of confidential information from an enclosed area may involve physical searches as well as the use of degaussers to wipe magnetic media clean.

Other physical hazards impacting the security of the environment include angels of fire which have the potential not only of destroying the information processing facility but also human life. Heat, smoke, noxious gases, and even damage from fire extinguishing systems, can all play a role in destroying the information processing facility. In general, fires require three things, namely:

- **Heat.** Fire starts where sufficient heat exists to ignite a fuel source. Heat can come from a variety of sources including deliberate intent, overloaded electrical systems, wrongly stored combustible material, and human carelessness.
- **Fuel source.** In a typical office environment fuels such as paper, plastic, wooden products, and the like are readily available but it should be borne in mind that, with an adequate supply of oxygen, almost anything will burn including steel and concrete.
- **Oxygen.** In order to maintain flame, fires require an ongoing source of oxygen. This may come in the form of a combustible material which itself contains sources of chemical oxygen so that simply smothering the fires to reduce oxygen in the air able to reach the heat source is ineffective. Nevertheless, the

readiest source of oxygen for a typical office fire is the air itself and open windows as well as air conditioning systems can accelerate the spread of a fire while the use of fire retardant materials and automatic shutoff mechanisms can slow the fire's progress.

Five preventative mechanisms work by denying the fire access to any or all of the three requirements for combustion. Most fire extinguishing systems such as halon, water-based, or carbon dioxide–based fire extinguishing systems will deny the fire access to both oxygen and heat. The fuel source itself may be denied simply by keeping the environment clean and removing threats such as overloaded electrical outlets.

In the event of a fire occurring, speed of detection can be critical to ensuring the fire is extinguished before significant damage to both property and personnel occurs. Fire can spread at a speed that surprises most people, and early detection, combined with some basic firefighting knowledge such as how to use an extinguisher, can quickly extinguish a small fire before it turns into a conflagration.

Given the vulnerability of computer systems and electronic equipment in general to sudden shifts in temperature as well as to water, care must be taken that extinguishing a computer fire does not cause more damage than the file itself.

Environmental Controls

Computer systems are, to a large extent, dependent upon the integrity of the physical environment within which they run. Modern computers are less susceptible to fluctuations in temperature and humidity, but loss of power is still a major risk area even for mobile devices. Use of dedicated power supplies, Uninterruptible Power Supply (UPS), and the use of standby generators can give consistency to power consumption.

Building collapse has long been a threat due to both natural and manmade threats. Long before the events at the World Trade Center brought structural collapse to management's attention, earth tremors, tornadoes, poorly built structures, and impacts at ground level cause structural collapse of offices containing computer centers. Preventative controls such as physical security combined with the proper sighting, design, and construction of buildings remain the strongest controls while, from a corrective perspective, appropriate and fully tested contingency plans are essential.

Logical Access Controls for the Identification,
Authentication, and Restriction of Users

Logical access is maintained via four critical concepts, namely:

- *Identification.* This could involve the identification of an individual by means of an access control mechanism such as the username or identification number as well as the identification of an external resource such as a network access, cloud access, or access via an external computer.
- *Authentication.* The mechanism by which a claimed identity might be proven. Authentication is normally carried out using something that the user has such as a token or digital certificate, knows, such as a password or the answer to a key question, or is using biometric authentication such as fingerprint scanning, iris scanning, facial recognition, and the like.
- *Authorization and Access Control.* This is a process by which rules are established and evaluated in order that an access control decision may be made, for example which level of staff is authorized to make changes to payment amounts on the payroll.
- *Monitoring.* Determining the extent of security logging required as well as the procedures to ensure that such monitoring takes place.

Risk and Controls Associated with Virtualization of Systems

The virtualization of systems within, for example, a cloud environment, has led some organizations to believe that they are inherently more secure than in a non-virtualized environment. Virtualization carries its own risks including the need for server virtualization security as well as network and storage virtualization security. These risks include:

- **VM Sprawl.**

  This term refers to the duplication of virtual machines on a network and, over a period of time, the duplicating machines may become neglected in terms of keeping security up to date and the operating environment current.

- **The existence of sensitive data within a VM environment.**

  In today's dynamic VMware environments, sensitive data has grown increasingly mobile, and is constantly being copied across a multiplicity of virtual machines and spread across the storage infrastructure, and over an increasingly diverse mix of physical platforms and operating systems. These complexities compel the organization to contend with additional layers of administrative privileges associated with the cloud provider's staff as well as guard against the potential for inadvertent or malicious access from other tenants within a multi-tenant cloud environment.

  This significantly increases the need for appropriate and effective encryption of all sensitive information.

- **Security of offline and dormant VMs.**

  One of the more significant loopholes in the implementation of virtualized systems deals with offline or dormant virtual machines. Virtual machines, by nature, can be created and populated dynamically whenever needed. In the same manner, virtual machines can also be suspended (made dormant) or brought offline based on the needs of the moment.

  As with VM Sprawl, security software updates and deployment of critical code patches stop happening. This renders such machines out of date for the period they are offline or dormant. As a result, when they are again brought online and provisioned, they exist in a singularity of vulnerability until their patches and software updates are brought up to date.

- **Lack of visibility and control over virtual networks.**

  Enforcing security policies can be problematic since traffic flowing via virtual networks may not be visible to devices such as intrusion-detection systems typically installed on a physical network. Because network traffic flowing between virtual machines does not originate at a particular host, the hypervisor is generally unable to monitor all communications happening between virtual machines.

- **Hypervisor security.**

  The hypervisor is a software layer residing between the underlying hardware platform and the virtual machines. The hypervisor is the program that controls the operation of the VMs. It is possible for a hacker to utilize entry points via the VMs themselves whereby malware that has infected one particular VM is able to penetrate the hypervisor and thus compromise other VMs that the hypervisor controls. Such risks can be mitigated by techniques such as:
  - Connecting only those physical devices that are currently being used
  - Finely tuning hypervisor configuration to disable high-risk activities such as memory sharing, file-sharing services, and clipboards between VMs running with the same hypervisor
  - Monitoring and analyzing hypervisor logs on a regular basis and utilizing appropriate hypervisor monitoring technologies
- **Account or service hijacking.**

  Cloud account hijacking is a process within which an individual or organization's cloud account is stolen or hijacked by an attacker. This is a common tactic utilized in identity theft schemes. The attacker uses the stolen account information to conduct malicious or unauthorized activity.

  At the enterprise level, this can be devastating, depending on what the attackers do with the information. Company integrity and reputations are at risk with confidential data potentially leaked or falsified resulting in significant cost to businesses or their customers. There may also be legal implications for companies and organizations in highly regulated industries, such as healthcare, where clients' or patients' confidential data may be exposed during cloud account hijacking incidents.
- **Multiple trust levels on the same server.**

  It is comparatively common to observe VMs with varying trust levels that are operated from the same physical server. As a result, VMs with lower trust levels will typically have security controls applied that are weaker than VMs with higher trust levels which potentially could leave possible pathways to compromise VMs with higher trust levels via VMs with lower trust levels.

Ideally, the organization should seek to run workloads of different trust levels on different physical or logical networks and servers, using firewalls to isolate high risk VM groups from other groups.

- **Risk due to cloud service providers APIs.**

   Service providers' application program interfaces (API) have created a powerful way for software applications to communicate and interact, but simultaneously their ease of use and ubiquity increases overall security risks. APIs are not in themselves a direct security threat. It is when an API end-user begins pulling data through requests, that security becomes an issue. APIs are utilized by a huge, and growing, variety of client devices – from traditional desktops to mobile devices, smart televisions, games consoles, and even nodes in the Internet of Things. Developers often do not provide enough boundaries to limit security problems in their efforts to encourage users and provide useful features.

   API security products are now available which can help minimize the attack potential presented by APIs.

Risks and Controls Associated with the Use of Mobile and Wireless Devices

Over the last ten years or so the use of mobile devices has exploded to the extent that, for many employees, use of mobile devices has become a way of life. The very portability of such devices makes authentication of the user of paramount importance. The use of passwords has always been problematic with users writing down passwords and using easily guessed passwords. Today many tablet devices and smartphones utilize biometric authentication techniques such as fingerprint scanning, facial recognition, voice recognition, and the like to boost the level of user authentication.

With the advent of usage analytics a user's individual pattern of use in terms of applications accessed, internet searches, social network usage, and even user mobility can create a pattern which, when varied, can identify potential anomalous usage and shut down access.

The fact still remains that security lies in the hands of the user, outside of the direct control of the organization. Data on such devices is commonly located in the cloud with the concomitant risks already discussed. As such, user education in IT security risks and their role in risk prevention and mitigation forms a critical control nexus.

Voice Communications Security

Phone hacking has been around for many years with electronic eavesdropping a reality both in the workplace and at home. With simple knowledge of the telephone number, voice conversations can be overheard and recorded and confidential information such as context data is readily obtainable for those with malicious intent. It is rapidly becoming essential that universal, end-to-end encryption is used for all voice communication if security is to be achieved.

Network and Internet Security Devices, Protocols, and Techniques

In today's world the internet has become the go-to workplace and social arena for many people. Internet Security Devices are in common use to detect viruses, malware, spyware, and the rest. Anti-malware systems have become non-negotiable to find and block malicious software and the selection of such systems will be dependent on the use for which it is intended.

Mobile Device Management (MDM) software is utilized with the company devices the organization has provided to employees which are specifically intended for work. This software is capable of introducing an additional security layer with remote monitoring. Remote locking is also achievable should a mobile device be lost, stolen, or strayed while remote erasure of data is also possible whether stored on a laptop, tablet, or phone.

In the home environment, the advent of the *Internet of Things* has brought a new level of risk with the need for router anti-malware and firewalls for network-connected devices and individual firewalls and devices connecting outside of the users' network control becoming essential.

Ultimately, it again goes down to user awareness of scams such as phishing attacks, attacks deriving from unsafe sites, and cultivation of an attitude of skepticism and wariness and the use of IT.

Configuration, Implementation, Operation, and Maintenance of Network Security Controls

As with all IT risk, it is not simply a case of going out and buying a package, loading it, switching it on, and instantly having security. Safeguarding the network's extended architecture, even in the home environment, involves a synchronization of multiple components. Security Information and Event Management (SIEM) systems allow the ongoing and real-time monitoring of log information from a variety of sources while Network Access Control (NAC) measures can assist in raising the level of control, the configuration and maintenance of such components can be a full-time job in a large network environment.

Encryption-Related Techniques and Their Uses

Cryptography is the name used to describe the use of mathematical algorithms to transform data from an understandable component into what appears to be garbage in such a way that the process can be reversed and the understandable data recovered. In IT, its primary use is as a protection of information in order to ensure data confidentiality, data integrity, user authentication, and the like.

Encryption is therefore a technique whereby a message or piece of data is rendered unreadable by scrambling up the data in such a way that a legitimate user can unscramble or *decrypt* the data easily but an unauthorized user would see only garbage. Not only does this technique maintain confidentiality of data but, should an attempt be made to corrupt the data while encrypted, the data would not decrypt, and the substitution would become apparent. Encryption does not prevent message destruction when used in network transmission, nor the knowledge of the fact that there *was* a message, albeit an unreadable one. It also has no impact on the accuracy and completeness of data or the timeliness of data transmission. Encryption is therefore only one of a variety of control techniques to be implemented.

The two fundamental components of any encryption system are the *algorithm* or mathematical formula and a *key*, a randomizer to reduce the possibility of letter-frequency analysis which may be used to attempt to crack encryption.

The key is introduced to the algorithm to randomize the production of the encrypted information (cyphertext). There are two primary types of key system, namely Single Key Systems (symmetric encryption), where one single key is used to both encrypt and decrypt data. Where, for example, a file is encrypted on a computer disk, this form of encryption can be highly effective. Where the purpose of encryption is to conceal the contents of a message sent between two individuals, this is less adequate because the same key must be known at both ends, the sender and receiver giving double the chance of a key becoming known. In such a situation at *two key* or *public key system* is normally more effective.

Public Key Infrastructure (PKI) Components and Digital Signature Techniques

A public key system utilizes two keys with one key (A) being used to encrypt a message while the other (B) can decrypt it. The process may be reversed using key B to encrypt and key A to decrypt. The strength of a public key system lies in the fact that a given message cannot be encrypted and decrypted using the same key.

Using this technique, the individual or organization can place one key (the public key) and the public domain while retaining the second key as a secret key. In this way any message sent to the individual would be encrypted using the public key. Anyone can look up the public key and send an encrypted message to the recipient, however only the recipient holds the private key and can decrypt a message.

Reversal of this technique gives the capability of using a digital signature where a clear text message can be encrypted with the private key which only the individual knows, the individual's identification is appended to the message, and the message sent. Any recipient can look up the individual's identification, seek the public key, and decrypt the message. Using this technique anyone can receive the message but only the originator could have sent it giving it an effective digital signature.

Public Key Infrastructure (PKI) is therefore a set of roles, policies, and procedures used to create, distribute, store, manage, and revoke digital certificates in order to adequately manage public-key encryption, allowing users and computers to securely exchange data over networks while verifying the identity of the other party.

Peer-to-Peer Computing, Instant Messaging, and Web-Based Technologies

In utilizing peer-to-peer (P2P) applications, the individual may be giving access to personal information to other users unintentionally. Once such information has been exposed, it becomes extremely difficult to ascertain how many and who has accessed it, increasing the exposure to identity theft risk.

In addition, certain applications may require the opening of specific ports on the firewall in order to facilitate file transfers and this again may expose vulnerabilities and allow an outsider to penetrate the firewall or even modify it.

Utilization of an appropriate firewall, properly configured, combined with anti-malware and anti-virus software can go a long way in reducing these exposures.

Instant Messaging (IM) is a real-time application that is rapidly replacing email as a method of passing quick messages. Within this context the major vulnerabilities lie at the door of the user since risks in this arena are commonly exposed in plain sight and are frequently ignored by users in the search for ease and speed of communications. In addition, IM is becoming the distribution mechanism of choice for viruses and worms since these messages may bypass traditional gateways and anti-virus security. Spoofing of IP addresses is facilitated in many public IM systems which allowed the creation of anonymous identities not mapping to email addresses.

Although most IM messages utilize standard ports, IM clients may also exploit open ports on the firewall used by other applications or use randomly negotiated ports. This has become known as *IM Tunneling*. File transfer using these techniques may permit the transfer of confidential information in an unmonitored way without content filtering.

IM has also opened the gateway to *Spim* (the instant messaging equivalent of spam) with the disruptive and legal risks, common to email spam.

Once again, it is critical that all employees must understand that the short IM message, apparently innocuous, sent to the wrong person or containing the wrong information can be extremely damaging to the organization and security awareness training becomes essential.

Data Classification Standards Related to the Protection of Information Assets

Data classification standards and frameworks used to assess data sensitivity, typically measured by the negative impact on the business that a breach of data would have thus facilitated the establishment of a protection profile requirement for each class of data. Such classification can be seen to be one of the critical components of any *Enterprise Information Security Policy* addressing the security of information maintained within Electronic Systems.

Within the standards data can be classified based on:

- Negative financial impact on the organization
- Damage to the reputation of the organization
- Loss of critical organizational capability
- Violation of legal or regulatory statute
- Statutory requirement for notification
- Violation of corporate policies plans and procedures

Controls designed and implemented for the protection of data must be mapped onto the level of identified risks pertaining to the creation, storage, transmission, and utilization of data. This classification becomes the responsibility of the Data Owner as well as the Data Manager and the Custodial Data Steward.

The data itself may be classified as:

- *Low sensitivity* – data available for routine public disclosure and use such as marketing material, annual reports, and information, which are not seen to be confidential although they may be sensitive to unauthorized manipulation or change.

- *Medium sensitivity* – internal data for use within the organization whose disclosure to third parties requires appropriate authorization.
- *High sensitivity* – such data are considered highly confidential and breach of such confidentiality, even within the organization, would be problematic. Loss of confidentiality of such data could seriously impact the reputation of the integrity of the organization.

Storage, Retrieval, Transportation, and Disposal of Confidential Information Assets

Assets which store data should be subject to adequate authorization controls that can identify the asset, its usage, and disposal in order to ensure security is maintained at all stages. It became apparent during the Y2K conversions that records of assets in many IT areas were deplorable and that disks, tapes, and even computers had disappeared without trace.

Disposal of confidential assets requires that, at a minimum, data should be removed utilizing low-level formatting, degaussing, or physical destruction prior to disposal.

Data Leakage

Data leakage may be defined as the unauthorized transfer of confidential information from computer or data center to external recipients. At its most basic, this may involve simply remembering what was seen on a screen through to application or operation systems weaknesses which reveal sensitive data such as security structures or user-specific data.

Perhaps the most common source of data loss involves hardware or system malfunctions acquiring the attention of individuals who may not normally be authorized to access classified confidential information. This is not, however, the only source of data leakage. Unauthorized access during data transmission as well as unauthorized access on internal networks are also threat sources, as are attacks by malicious outsiders intruding into the organizational infrastructure in order to steal accumulated data about employees, clients, or business financial data. In many organizations, sensitive data is maintained in encrypted form on storage mediums. Such data becomes decrypted when it appears on screens and in browsers where it becomes sensitive to electronic eavesdropping. This can leave the organization open to theft of intellectual property.

Risks in End-User Computing

Systems Performance

Computing as a technique has been around since the advent of the microcomputer and tools such as VisiCalc (the first electronic spreadsheet) became popular on Apple II PCs. In its early days, end-user computing (EUC) was primarily used as a calculator replacement with the normal risks of inaccuracy and operator finger trouble. Over time such tools have become ubiquitous in the workplace and are being used for major business applications. When systems were designed for running under an IT-controlled environment, the SDLC ensured that adequate controls were designed-in, testing was carried out to a professional standard and ongoing maintenance was properly controlled.

In many EUC implementations, the designers are inadequately trained, controls vary depending on the skill of the end-user, adequate testing is commonly omitted, change control is ignored, and the security aspects are frequently overlooked. As part of the IT risk management process, the security aspects and extent of EUC utilization within the organization must be considered. With modern technology, the business risk of not implementing EUC is substantial and the continuing growth in EUC cannot be ignored. Once again, control aspects in this area evolve and the shoulders of the users and adequate training and awareness must be enforced.

Implementing a Security Awareness Program

Security as a whole goes beyond simply a technical problem. It is an organizational problem with a technical component, as well as a human component. The overall goal of the security awareness program is to operate on the human component so as to raise the probability of effective implementation of security best practices.

As with all control structures, IT security is dependent on the ability and willingness of those tasked with exercising control to carry out those tasks in an effective manner. Security is the responsibility of all employees of the organization. The overall security awareness program consists of four components, namely:

- Communication throughout the organization on an ongoing basis to ensure that security awareness is maintained across all areas.
- The security architecture outlining IT risks with role-based guidelines appropriate for individual IT users. This may take the form of a corporate IT security handbook.
- Ongoing security awareness training in order to keep IT security at the forefront of the individual's thought processes. Such training need not be based on formal education courses but may incorporate such training activities as 'storytelling' regarding the good and bad corporate experiences of failures of IT security. Security awareness training should at a minimum be conducted for new employees, for all employees after an incident has occurred, and on an ongoing basis throughout the year.
- Detective controls are required as part of IT security awareness. Preventative controls are never 100% effective and for IT security to be implemented on an ongoing basis, employees must be able to recognize when preventative controls have failed and understand their role and what happens next.

Information System Attack Methods and Techniques

Many of the attack methods have already been covered in this book but include:

- Malware
- Phishing
- Pharming
- Password attacks
- Denial of Service (DoS) attacks
- 'Man in the Middle'(MITM) attacks
- Drive-by downloads
- Rogue software

- Ransomware
- Spyware and adware
- Social engineering

Prevention and Detection Tools and Control Techniques

Each of these attack techniques requires a combination of preventative and detective controls in order to obviate the threat.

Malware

That term is an all-inclusive description for a variety of threats including viruses, Trojans, and worms. In essence, malware is code which is introduced with malicious intent to steal or destroy information on a computer system. Preventing malware is easier said than done. Prevention of activating links or the downloading of attachments from subversive senders may be assisted by the effective use of firewalls, but ultimately such prevention lies in the hands of the user.

Phishing

As previously noted, phishing requires a response to a request for information from a 'trusted' third party requesting confidential information often under the guise of preventing the user been cut off from a desired resource.

Again, it is easy to say 'do not respond', but the reality is that today's phishing attacks have become more sophisticated over the years and independent verification of the source of the request has become problematic. Many organizations, such as the IRS, warn consumers that they will not ask for personal information in a manner which could be confused with the phishing attack. Even if a request recommends independent confirmation by phoning a given number, the number given is suspect and needs to be independently verified.

Pharming

This type of attack involves the redirection of a website's traffic to a fake site where a user's information can be compromised. This type of attack may consist of either exploitation of a vulnerability in Domain Name Server (DNS) software or changing the host files in the attacked computer. The origination of such an attack is commonly via an email introducing a virus to attack the user's local DNS cache. This form of attack is difficult to detect since there is no requirement for the victims to respond to a message, however should such an attack be suspected, restarting the computer may reset the local DNS entries and access may be again attempted to the website. This response is not infallible as it depends on whether the attack has been at the local end or at the central DNS server.

Password Attacks

And password attack is, as its name suggests, an attempt by a third party to gain access to the organization's computer by simply cracking the user's password. Multiple password cracking programs exist using dictionary checking techniques or simply brute force attacks trying every possible combination of letters and characters until access is gained.

The technical solution is to move to an authentication method which does not require passwords such as facial recognition, fingerprint scanning, or other biometric techniques.

The non-technical solution involves the user making use of strong passwords involving combinations of upper- and lower-case letters combined with numbers and symbols of an extended length, and changing them frequently for words or phrases not commonly found in dictionaries.

Denial of Service (DoS) Attacks

A Denial of Service attack combined with a Distributed Denial of Service (DDoS) attack involves disrupting a network typically by sending high volumes of traffic such that the network becomes overloaded and can no longer function. This is most commonly found in large organizations targeted by outside groups of attackers usually as some form of protest.

Prevention of such attacks involves maintaining a high level of security within the system by, for example, monitoring data flow to identify unusual spikes in traffic, real-time security monitoring, and regular updates of Security Software and operating system patches.

This assumes that such an attack would take a logical form, however physical DoS attacks may be successful simply by disconnecting a server from the network by pulling the plug.

'Man in the Middle' (MITM) attacks

A MITM attack takes the form of impersonating both of the endpoints in a communication such that the user may believe, for example, that they are communicating directly with their bank, while the bank is under the impression that they are talking directly to the user. In this event all of the user's information is transmitted to the MITM, copied or altered, and forwarded to the bank. The bank's reply would again be transmitted via the MITM who would then have access to sensitive information. This is an example in a banking application but is equally applicable wherever confidential communication is essential.

Access in such attacks is commonly via a non-encrypted wireless access point and the most effective defense is the use of only high-quality encrypted access points when wireless communication is being used. Where confidential communication is essential, use of Virtual Private Networks (VPNs) should be considered.

Drive-By Downloads

Where a user accesses a compromised website, a piece of malware may automatically download to the user's system, opening a back door through which other, more sophisticated malware may be downloaded without user intervention. In many such cases the website accessed as a legitimate website and that the user has no way of knowing that it has been compromised.

In addition to the use of anti-malware software, browser add-ons with security implications should be minimized, switched off, or disabled.

Rogue Software

This is a term given to malware which masquerades as legitimate software (commonly, security software). It is downloaded when alerts are generated advising the user to download 'latest versions', or agree to terms in order to stay secure. By clicking on 'Yes' the malware is then downloaded.

As with other malware attacks, user vigilance combined with up-to-date firewall, anti-virus, anti-spyware, and anti-malware software should help reduce the likelihood of successful attacks in this area.

Ransomware

Ransomware is a form of malicious software which threatens to publish the user's data or, alternatively, blocks the user's access to their own data unless a ransom is paid. Introduction of ransomware is commonly through phishing and other e-mail scams with access being blocked using encryption. Data will only be decrypted once a ransom has been paid. A variation involving threatening to publish data is also known as *leakware* and is generally directed at organizations where loss of confidentiality could threaten the ongoing viability or reputation of the organization attacked.

Prevention of such attacks again comes down to keeping operating systems patched and up to date as well as blocking the installation of software without explicit knowledge of where it came from and how it was authorized. Maintaining adequate backups will not prevent such an attack but may, in the case of access denial, mitigate the impact of such an attack.

Spyware and Adware

Spyware may be defined as software which installs on a computer and generally tracks web usage so that pop-up adverts may be targeted directly at the individual. The software may also attempt to redirect home pages to specific sites and may block access to sites offering competing products. In some cases, the spyware may be introduced via a legitimate software installation where the user's click of the 'next' button will install the software as an add-on. Many such software installations come via peer-to-peer file-sharing services where the spyware is installed during the networking installation procedure.

Social Engineering

This technique involves the use of deception in order to influence individuals to divulge confidential or personal information to enable password attacks or ID theft.

Destruction of confidential waste and user alertness form the two major defenses against social engineering. The object of the exercise is to keep confidential information out of the hands of the outsider.

Security Testing Techniques

Security testing is carried out to determine how vulnerable a system may be and to determine the extent of protection implemented to prevent access by potential intruders. This involves the revealing of flaws and security mechanisms as well as finding vulnerabilities within software applications.

Security testing normally starts with a review of the security architecture in order to determine the business requirements, security objectives, and control opportunities in terms of the risk appetite of the organization. Data would typically be collected on all System Software and Network Software in order to identify potential vulnerabilities. Based on this information, a threat profile would be established in order to determine the vulnerabilities and security risks together with the internal control structures intended to guard against such risks. This, then, forms the basis of the design of a testing plan in order to determine the effectiveness and efficiency of the control architecture intended to mitigate the risks.

Certain of the controls may be manually executed and can be tested accordingly, however some will require the use of a selected security testing tool in order to simulate attack scenarios. Such tools need to be tailored based upon the selected education for the individual organization and the selected controls implemented.

Penetration Testing and Vulnerability Scanning

Penetration testing is an attempt to actively exploit weaknesses identified within an environment while vulnerability scanning involves the assessment of systems against a list of known vulnerabilities.

Automated tools commonly used for vulnerability scanning and involve such tasks as:

- Scanning for missing vendor patches within internal networks
- Scanning external networks for known vulnerabilities

Penetration testing is commonly carried out by specialist organizations using exploit code as required to attempt to get beyond the implemented internal control structures. One variation on penetration testing is the use of 'ethical hackers' who will attempt to use the tools and techniques in common use by the hacking community to penetrate the organization's systems.

Monitoring and Responding to Security Incidents

At all times it is essential that the organization stays abreast of the latest incidents of security penetration on an international basis and incorporates such incidents into its own monitoring of the security environment. Any red flags indicating potential security incidents within the organization require immediate alert and response from the appropriate authority within the organization.

Forensic Investigation and Procedures in Collection and Preservation of the Data and Evidence

Any investigation must minimize business disruption. Gathering of forensically acceptable evidence will commonly involve isolating the information source to prevent contamination. In the case of Information Systems, such isolation, if extended over a period of time, could result in considerably more damage to the organization than the original fraud or security failure.

Once gathered, the evidence must be such that would allow for legal recrimination. This means that the evidence must be capable of standing up to public scrutiny and challenge.

Mandia and Prosise* define an incident response methodology as incorporating:

---

* Kevin Mandia and Chris Prosise: Incident Response—Investigating Computer Crime, Berkeley, California: Osborne/McGraw-Hill, 2001, pp. 16–17.

- Pre-incident preparation
- Detection of incidents
- Initial response
- Response strategy formulation
- Duplication (forensic backups)
- Investigation
- Security measure implementation
- Network monitoring
- Recovery
- Reporting
- Follow-up

Once a working copy of the data is available, the forensic investigator must decide what evidence is to be sought. Depending on the nature of the investigation, files accessed, emails sent and received, internet sites visited, programs executed, and graphic files accessed may all be of interest to the investigator.

In its simplest form, an investigator seeking evidence of the presence on the computer of illicit or illegal files or software may simply have to do a search for a specific file name or file type. Even this may be complicated if the files concerned have been deleted and the investigator may have to resurrect such deleted files prior to examination.

Where fraud has occurred, the files accessed, date and time of access, network paths taken, and software executed may be critical.

Modern operating systems have the capacity to record such accesses. Log files and registry entries can contain such information as usernames, passwords, recently accessed files, and network connections used. Unfortunately, having the capacity does not necessarily mean that such records are created and retained. Once again, the investigator will have to search for such files, possibly now deleted, before they can be interrogated.

Domain 5 – Practice Questions

1. Possibly one of the most significant aspects of computer security is its capacity to protect us from the effects of:
   a. Breakdowns of physical security.
   b. Our own mistakes.

    c. Computer disasters.

    d. Computer fraud.

2. A breakdown in information system security could result in:

    a. Employees selling confidential data to competitors or others.

    b. Self-insurance proving too expensive.

    c. IT department's security goals being incompatible with the organization's.

    d. The gap between computer technology and computer security widening.

3. The three basic principles governing computer security are:

    a. Integrity, confidentiality, and completeness.

    b. Confidentiality, security, and completeness.

    c. Confidentiality, security, and availability.

    d. Integrity, confidentiality, and availability.

4. A computer virus causing changes to information held within computer systems would be a failure of:

    a. Integrity.

    b. Confidentiality.

    c. Availability.

    d. Integrity, confidentiality. and availability.

5. Selection of the appropriate control techniques is dependent upon:

    a. Cost.

    b. Availability of resources.

    c. Management's perception of vulnerabilities and threats.

    d. Quality of the IS auditor.

6. Logical security is involved in determining:

    a. The identity of users.

    b. Users' right of access.

    c. The authenticity of users.

    d. All of the above.

7. A technique using mathematical algorithms to transform data is known as:

    a. Steganography.

b. Cryptanalysis.
c. Encryption.
d. Steganalysis.

8. An encryption technique using two keys is known as:
   a. Symmetrical encryption.
   b. Asymmetrical encryption.
   c. DES.
   d. Steganography.

9. One disadvantage to symmetric encryption is the fact that:
   a. Both ends of communication must know the same key.
   b. It is more expensive than asymmetric encryption.
   c. It is more difficult to reverse than asymmetric encryption.
   d. It is easier to use than asymmetric encryption.

10. A message authentication code can be derived from:
    a. Key fields only.
    b. All transmitted data.
    c. Either key fields or all transmitted data.
    d. Neither key fields nor all transmitted data.

11. Double public key cryptography is used to achieve:
    a. Security of information.
    b. Authentication of transmitter.
    c. Authentication of receiver.
    d. End-to-end message authentication.

12. The concealing of information within another file is known as:
    a. Symmetrical encryption.
    b. Asymmetrical encryption.
    c. DES.
    d. Steganography.

13. Steganography can work to the organization's advantage by:
    a. Concealing an electronic 'watermark' on copyrighted material.
    b. Concealing pirate copies of software.
    c. Concealing unauthorized images.
    d. Concealing illegal transactions.

14. An information security policy providing the fundamental guidelines used in assessing the value of information assets must spell out in detail:
    a. Access is granted to individuals only to perform their business function.
    b. Employees must keep the organization's information assets secure even if it means breaking the law.
    c. Data confidentiality must be achieved at all costs.
    d. Data integrity must be achieved at all costs.

15. Operating systems are intended to:
    a. Facilitate the operation of a computer on an ongoing basis from application program to application program with minimal operator intervention.
    b. Permit each computer to be operated as a unique machine under the direct control of the systems designers and programmers.
    c. Manage the basic functionality of the computer and a unique format for each machine.
    d. Facilitate the interoperability of a variety of machines via one single network.

16. An operating system intended to serve the requests of client computers on the network is:
    a. A mainframe operating system.
    b. An embedded operating system.
    c. A server operating system.
    d. A PC operating system.

17. Operating systems are tailored by selecting among potential alternatives using:
    a. The registry.
    b. Parameters.
    c. User appendages.
    d. Utilities.

18. The IS auditor should ensure that the operating system:
    a. Operates in an efficient manner.
    b. Is controlled only by the operators.

c. Does not use default accounts and passwords.

d. Is tailored only by IT management.

19. Auditing the operating system will normally involve:

a. Examining the coding of the operating system.

b. Ensuring the internal controls within the operating environment function as intended.

c. Browsing the operating environment with CAATs.

d. Examining the log files going back for the preceding year.

20. Information systems security is designed to provide support for:

a. Management.

b. Users.

c. External auditors.

d. All of the above.

21. RACF, ACF2, and Top Secret are examples of:

a. Librarian systems.

b. Security systems.

c. Network operating systems.

d. Standard utilities.

22. User authentication can be accomplished by:

a. Something the user is.

b. Something the user has.

c. Something the user knows.

d. All of the above.

23. Passwords suffer from which major drawback when:

a. They're hard to guess.

b. They're frequently changed.

c. Users must remember their password.

d. Users must write the password down.

24. One disadvantage of biometric authentication is that:

a. The user may not be able to change it if it is compromised.

b. No authentication method is foolproof.

c. They do not protect privacy or prevent the taking over of a session.

d. All of the above.

25. Backdoors are:
    a. Useful for the systems programmer to issue operator commands without going through security.
    b. Software loopholes accidentally left in systems to permit entry in an unauthorized manner.
    c. Useful for the systems programmer to modify the operating system without restarting the computer.
    d. Normally kept hidden and only used when needed.

26. A major problem of a peripheral defense over a network is:
    a. The presumption that once inside the network a user has that right to be there.
    b. Peripheral defenses only address the internal threats.
    c. The large number of entry points into a network.
    d. All of the above.

27. Network security breaches can lead to:
    a. Loss of reputation.
    b. User authentication failure.
    c. System unavailability.
    d. All of the above.

28. A network area containing information resources opened to the public but requiring user identification and authentication is:
    a. A hostile zone.
    b. An untrusted zone.
    c. A semi-trusted zone.
    d. A trusted zone.

29. Sniffer software can result in:
    a. Loss of reputation.
    b. User authentication failure.
    c. Loss of confidentiality.
    d. All of the above.

30. Default system accounts and passwords should be:
    a. Left alone.
    b. Removed if not in use.
    c. Removed whenever possible.
    d. Removed only if the corporate security policy requires it.

31. Access rights should be granted:
    a. To everyone.
    b. To anyone who asks for it.
    c. To anyone who needs to have it.
    d. To anyone whose manager asks for it.

32. Client-server systems are different from ordinary systems in that:
    a. Functionality and processing of a system are split between the workstation and the database server.
    b. Functionality and processing of this system are duplicated on both the workstation and database server.
    c. The client and server are separated logically but not physically.
    d. The client and server are separated physically but not logically.

33. A firewall can be used as:
    a. A preventative control.
    b. A detective control.
    c. A directive control.
    d. All of the above.

34. A security drawback of a solitary firewall access route is that:
    a. It may become overloaded.
    b. It may be difficult to administer.
    c. In may block a service that, sooner or later, the user will wish to use.
    d. There may be no protection from the insider threats behind a firewall.

35. Digital signatures are used to:
    a. Conceal the contents of a message.
    b. Confirm the authenticity of the sender of a message.
    c. Confirm the authenticity of the receiver of a message.
    d. All of the above.

36. Digital certificates are used to certify:
    a. An organization's or individual's private key.
    b. An organization's or individual's public key.

   c. An organization's or individual's private and public keys.

   d. An organization's or individual's privileges within any system.

37. IDSs may detect intrusions based on:
   a. Statistical anomaly detection.
   b. A database of common attack patterns.
   c. Deviations from expected behavior.
   d. All of the above.

38. Accidental physical damage could be a result of:
   a. Malicious destruction.
   b. A fire.
   c. A hacker.
   d. All of the above.

39. Handing over malfunctioning equipment to outside experts could result in:
   a. Theft of equipment.
   b. Loss of confidentiality.
   c. Physical damage and destruction.
   d. All of the above.

40. Card locks are more vulnerable to:
   a. Sharing of cards between multiple individuals.
   b. Physical security of the card.
   c. Observation of the unlocking process.
   d. One person opening the door and three people entering.

41. Fire requires:
   a. Heat, fuel source, ignition.
   b. Fuel source, oxygen, ignition.
   c. Heat, oxygen, ignition.
   d. Heat, fuel source, oxygen.

42. Sprinkler systems are:
   a. A bad idea because of the water damage.
   b. A good idea because the limit the spread of a fire.
   c. A bad idea because the fire must have started before they take effect.
   d. A good idea because they remove the fuel source.

43. A UPS is an appropriate control for:
   a. Fire prevention.
   b. Fire detection.
   c. Disaster recovery planning.
   d. Ensuring continuity of power.

44. The most effective corrective control in the event of a building collapse is:
   a. The corporate contingency plan.
   b. The computer disaster recovery plan.
   c. Well-built buildings.
   d. All of the above.

Domain 5 – Review Questions and Hands-On Exercise

- Describe the fundamental concepts underlying Information Assets Security.
- Explain the major business problems which the failure of information security can lead to.
- Describe the major forms of encryption and message authentication.
- Describe the major problem areas to be found in encryption processes.
- Define the main components of an information security policy.
- Describe the fundamental concepts governing Computer Operating Systems.
- Explain how tailoring the Operating System affects security.
- Identify the steps in auditing operating environments.
- Define the components of logical IT security, logical access control issues, and exposures, access control software.
- Describe the role of security packages.
- Describe the logical security risks, controls, and audit considerations (audit of logical access, security testing) together with logical security features, tools, procedures.
- Explain the need for and basic processes in ensuring Logical Computer Security.
- Describe the techniques of user authentication.

- Explain the need for communications and network security.
- Identify and describe the principles of network security.
- Explain the impact of client-server, and other services.
- Describe the usage and types of firewall security systems and other connectivity protection resources (e.g. cryptography, digital signatures, key management policies).
- Define the nature of intrusion detection systems.
- Describe the environmental issues and exposures concepts and their effect on physical IT security.
- Identify appropriate physical access exposures and controls.
- Identify the primary threat areas within a paperless environment.
- Determine the changes to the internal control structure required in such an environment.
- Identify the new sources of audit and legal evidence.
- Identify deficiencies within their current audit approaches.
- Design and implement a corrective program to bring the audit program in line with the changing business environment.
- Identify the major threats and controls regarding identity theft.

Exercise 5

CBSINC, a retail organization, needed assurance that its sensitive information was protected against hackers and other internet threats. CBSINC management was concerned about compliance-related issues and wanted assurance its systems were protected against external threats.

In conducting a Cyber Security review, what would the audit program consist of and what types of tools would the auditor use?

Exercise 5 Sample Answer

Audit services would include:

- Firewall – review and analyze configuration
- External penetration – evaluate vulnerabilities
- Social engineering – determine employee risks

- Phishing – use fake emails and USB devices to test resilience
- Compare CBSINC with industry benchmarks and determine the type of security infrastructure in place
- Policies – evaluate security-related policies and test the effectiveness of controls implemented

CAATs would include a variety of hacker-type tools and techniques that identify and evaluate CBSINC's external and internal risks including password crackers, log analyzers, and network vulnerability scanners.

Domain 5 – Answers to Practice Questions

1. **B** Since most computer problems arise from human error, the most significant aspect of Computer Security disability to protect us from the impact of our own mistakes.
2. **A** This is the only option which could *result* from a breakdown in Information Systems Security. The rest are all potential causes of a breakdown.
3. **D** While all of these are important, the basic principles laid down in COBIT® are integrity, confidentiality, and availability.
4. **A** Unauthorized changes to information from whichever source is a failure of integrity. Changes to data would not necessarily affect confidentiality or availability.
5. **C** In all cases, decisions on the appropriate control techniques are dependent on the vulnerability and threats within the environment as perceived by management.
6. **D** Logical security starts off with the identification of users, ensuring that the user is who they claim to be (authenticity), and determining the user's right of access.
7. **C** Data transformation from clear text to cyphertext is done by encryption using mathematical algorithms.
8. **B** Symmetrical encryption uses a single key to encrypt and decrypt. DES, the data encryption standard, is a symmetrical key encryption process. Steganography involves the concealment of the fact that a message exists and asymmetrical encryption uses a two key system.

9. **A** Symmetric encryption is where one key is used to encrypt and the same key is used to decrypt, both ends of communication must know the same key leaving an exposure at each end to inadvertent or deliberate leakage of the key.

10. **C** Depending on the method used, a message authentication code may be derived from any combination of data selected.

11. **D** Public key cryptography is designed to ensure security of information by encrypting with the public key such that only the holder of the private key can decrypt. By reversing the process and encrypting with the private key any receiver can decrypt but only the originator could have encrypted. Double public key encryption provides end-to-end authentication since only the authorized transmitter could have encrypted and only the authorized recipient could have decrypted.

12. **D** Concealment of a message within another message or within a file is achieved using steganography, the technique of hiding secret data within an ordinary, non-secret file or message.

13. **A** Only the first answer is an advantage. The other three answers indicate potential disadvantages.

14. **A** The information security policy must spell out the circumstances under which access is granted to individuals. It cannot advocate breaking the law nor specify that security must be achieved *at all costs*. There are few circumstances where cost of control does not need to be taken into consideration.

15. **A** This is the generic definition of an operating system.

16. **C** A server operating system is classified as an operating system designed to serve the requests of client computers on a network.

17. **B** Operating systems, like most software packages where alternative processing options may be selected, are tailored by managerial selection of alternative parameters.

18. **C** One common failing of the tailoring of operating systems is the tendency to leave accounts and passwords supplied with a system unchanged. Since many of these default accounts and passwords and detailed in the systems documentation, the auditor should ensure that these are changed.

19. **B** Operating systems typically run to many millions of lines of code and are kept as confidential propriety information unavailable to the auditors. Although referred to as auditing the operating system, the auditors typically examine the internal controls implemented within the operating environment to ensure they function as intended using a variety of audit techniques.

20. **D** Information Systems Security is intended for use in support of all stakeholders in the IT process.

21. **B** These are examples of Security Systems designed to operate within the IBM Z/OS operating environment.

22. **D** Any of these individually or in combination can assist in the authentication that a user is who they claim to be.

23. **C** Because users must remember the password, common words, or easily guessed passwords that are frequently used. Passwords should be hard to guess and frequently changed although not written down.

24. **A** The biggest problem in using biometric authentication techniques is that they are based on something unique to the user which cannot be easily duplicated (good) and cannot be changed (bad). If, for example, a digitized fingerprint is copied, there is no way for the user to change their fingerprint.

25. **B** Back doors are typically unauthorized coding placed within systems during development to facilitate ease of access by the programmer. They are intended to be kept secret and used only when needed but, if not removed in a live system, and a loophole has been left which can permit entry in an unauthorized manner.

26. **A** Peripheral defenses, whether physical or logical, suffer from the same weakness that, should the periphery be penetrated, it is assumed that anyone within the periphery has a right to be there.

27. **D** Security breaches within a network can be caused by user authentication failure and can potentially lead to loss of reputation or system unavailability.

28. **C** An un-trusted zone refers to an external system, such as the internet, not owned by the organization. Such systems may also be seen as hostile zones. A semi-trusted zone refers to an

externally exposed system containing public data. A trusted zone is internally exposed only.

29. **D** Sniffer software is designed to eavesdrop on a network so that all or selected information flowing may be viewed or duplicated. As such, the potential is for all of the above failures.

30. **C** Default system accounts and passwords leave a vulnerability within the system and should be removed whenever possible. The maintenance contract with the software supplier may require the default accounts and passwords be retained in case of emergency access requirement. This should be negotiated with vendors wherever possible.

31. **C** All computer access rights should be granted on a need-to-have basis wherever possible.

32. **A** The major differentiation in a client-server system is that the actual functionality and processing of the application system are divided between the workstation and the server.

33. **D** Firewalls may be configured to prevent unauthorized access, to detect attempts at unauthorized access, and to compel adherence to corporate rules and regulations regarding access. As such they may fulfill all three roles.

34. **D** Where access is achieved via a solitary firewall, the firewall acts as a peripheral defense and security may be compromised by those operating within the firewall.

35. **B** Digital signatures are a form of asynchronous encryption used to confirm the authenticity of the sender of a message. They do not conceal the contents of the message and do not act to ensure the authenticity of the receiver of a message.

36. **B** In a Public Key Infrastructure (PKI)environment, digital certificates are means by which an organization or individual's public key may be derived so that communication may be authenticated.

37. **D** Intrusion Detection Systems (IDSs) will analyze communication patterns and detect intrusions based on anomalous deviations or common attack patterns.

38. **B** Physical damage could come about as a result of malicious destruction or fire, but malicious destruction is not accidental. Hacking does not normally result in physical damage.

39. **D** History has shown that, although sometimes essential, handing over malfunctioning equipment has occasionally led to the theft of equipment, physical damage and, where confidential data still exists on a computer, loss of confidentiality is possible.

40. **B** Card locks face a variety of vulnerabilities but the loss of the card itself may invalidate the whole process.

41. **D** The three main ingredients required for a fire are heat, a fuel source, and a source of oxygen. The oxygen may be provided from the air or within a chemical process.

42. **C** Where used, modern sprinkler systems use demineralized water and are synchronized with power cut off devices to minimize water damage. Unfortunately, sprinkler systems typically only trigger after a fire has started and reached sufficient heat to activate the sprinkler heads.

43. **C** An Uninterruptible Power Supply (UPS) is designed to ensure continuity of Power Supply in the event of the main power being terminated.

44. **A** Well-built buildings do not assist once a building has collapsed and the damage may go well beyond the Computer System. This would normally be catered for within the corporate contingency plan.

PREPARING FOR THE EXAMINATION

From past experience running CISA preparation courses, my recommendation is to spend 40% of your time ensuring your theoretical knowledge is up-to-date by studying the texts such as the *ISACA Candidate Information Guide*. The other 60% of your time should involve practicing the examination questions to come to terms with the ways questions are phrased to arrive at the correct answer. The focus should be on both the questions the candidate got wrong as well as those a candidate got right by accident. Guessing correctly may be acceptable if a candidate can be sure they would guess the same way in the examination and the wording of the question in the examination is the same as the one the candidates practice on.

A common tripping point is to encounter a question in practice which says 'what is the most', and encounter the same question in the examination but phrased 'what is not the most' or even 'what is the least'. Because the scenario is one the candidate has practiced, that is a temptation to say 'I remember this question, I know the answer' and pick the answer which was correct *in practice* but is wrong in the examination.

In preparation, I have found it very effective for groups of candidates to get together once a week for two-hour practice sessions where questions can be attempted, answers debated, and candidates get the opportunity to question others with differing backgrounds and knowledge based on misread, misunderstood, or just plain 'don't know' questions. My suggestion is that these study groups start no earlier than ten weeks out from the examination so that candidates hit the exam fully prepared but without going 'over the top'.

I wish you all the best in the examination and wait to welcome you to the CISA ranks.

In addition to the practice questions within this book, the ISACA website has a collection of free resources for CISA candidates including:

- Exam Candidate Information Guide[*]
- CISA Self-Assessment Exam[†]
- ISACA's Knowledge and Insights database of free papers[‡]

In Appendix B I have included 175 CISA-type questions which can be used to assemble sets of practice examinations to assist the candidate. The answers are in Appendix C.

---

[*] http://www.isaca.org/certification/pages/candidates-guide-for-exams.aspx

[†] http://www.isaca.org/Certification/CISA-Certified-Information-Systems-Auditor/Prepare-for-the-Exam/Pages/CISA-Self-Assessment.aspx

[‡] http://www.isaca.org/Knowledge-Center/Pages/default.aspx

APPENDICES

Appendix A

Glossary of Terms

Abend: An abnormal end to a computer job. Termination of a task prior to its completion because of an error condition that cannot be resolved by recovery facilities while the task is executing.

Access Control: The process which limits and controls access to resources of a computer system. A logical or physical control designed to protect against unauthorized entry or use.

Access Control Table: An internal computerized table of access rules regarding the levels of computer access permitted to logon-IDS and computer terminals.

Access Method: The technique used for selecting records in a file, one at a time, for processing, retrieval, or storage. The access method is related to, but distinct from, the file organization which determines how the records are stored.

Access Path: The logical route an end-user takes to access computerized information. Typically includes a route through the operating system, telecommunications software, selected application software, and the access control system.

Access Rights: Also called permissions or privileges. These are the rights granted to users by the administrator or supervisor. Access rights determine the actions users can perform – for example, Read, Write, Execute, Create, Delete – on files in shared volumes or file shared on the server.

Address: The code used to designate the location of a specific piece of data within computer storage.

Addressing: The method used to identify the location of a participant in a network. Ideally, addressing specifies where the participant is located rather than who they are (name) or how to get there (routing).

Address Space: The number of distinct locations that may be referred to with the machine address. For most binary machines it is equal to 2n, where n is the number of bits in the machine address.

Administrative Controls: Controls dealing with operational effectiveness, efficiency, and adherence to management policies.

Analog: A transmission signal that varies continuously in amplitude and time and is generated in wave formation. Analog signals are used in telecommunications.

Anonymous File Transfer Protocol (FTP): A method for downloading public files using the File Transfer Protocol (FTP). Anonymous FTP is called anonymous because the user does not need to identify him or herself before accessing files from a particular server. In general, one enters the word 'anonymous' when the host prompts for a username. Then the user can enter anything for the password, such as an email address or simply the word 'guest'. In many cases, when access is an anonymous FTP site, one will not even be prompted for a name and password.

Anti-Virus Software: Anti-virus software are anti-viral infection applications that detect, prevent, and log all known viruses to a micro-computer hard drive, Word, Excel, or email documents as well as diskettes. As a general standard, anti-virus software should be updated by vendors at least once a quarter. Examples of anti-virus software are McAfee and Norton.

Application Layer: A layer within the ISO International Standards Organization (ISO)/OSI model. It is related to the information transfers among users through application programs and other devices. In this layer various protocols are needed. Some of them are specific to certain applications and others are general for network services.

Application Program: A program that processes business data such as data entry, update, or query. Contrasts with systems programs, such as an operating system or network control program. Also contrasts with utility programs, such as 'copy' or 'sort'.

Application Programming: The act or function of developing and maintaining applications programs in 'production'.

Arithmetic-Logic-Unit (ALU): The area of the central processing unit that performs mathematical and analytical operations.

Artificial Intelligence: Advanced computer systems that can simulate human capabilities such as analysis based on a predetermined set of rules.

ASCII (American Standard Code for Information Interchange): An 8 digit/7 bit code representing 128 characters. Used in most small computers.

Assembler: A program that takes as input, a program written in assembly language, and translates it into machine code or relocatable code.

Assembly Language: A low-level computer programming language which uses symbolic code and produces machine language instructions.

Asymmetric Key (Public Key): A cipher technique whereby different cryptographic keys are used to encrypt ('scramble') a message.

Asynchronous Transmission: Character-at-a-time transmission.

Audit Objective: The specific goal(s) of an audit. These often center around substantiating the existence of internal controls to minimize business risk.

Audit Program: A step-by-step set of audit procedures and instructions that should be performed to complete an audit. The Audit Program also should be a guide for documenting the various audit steps performed and for pointing out the location of evidence in the audit workpapers.

Audit Risk: The risk that information or financial reports may contain material errors that the auditor may not detect.

Audit Trail: A visible trail of evidence enabling one to trace information contained in statements or reports back to the original input source.

Authentication: The act of verifying the identity of a user and the user's eligibility to access computerized information. Designed to protect against fraudulent logon activity. Authentication can also refer to the verification of the correctness of a piece of data.

Asynchronous Transfer Mode (ATM): An ATM is a high-bandwidth low-delay switching and multiplexing technology. It is a Data Link Layer Protocol. This means that it is a protocol-independent transport mechanism. ATM allows integration of Frame Relay, SMDS, and circuit emulation. ATMs are very high speed at up to 10 Gb/s, permanent point-to-point connection, and require fiber optic connection.

Automated Teller Machine (ATM): An ATM is a 24-hour, stand-alone mini-bank, located outside branch bank offices or in public places like shopping malls. Through ATMs, clients can access deposits, withdrawals, account inquiries, and transfers. Typically, the ATM network is comprised of two spheres; a proprietary sphere, in which the bank manages the transactions of its clients, and the public or shared domain, in which a client of one financial institution can use another's ATMs.

Backup: Files, equipment, data, and procedures available for use in the event of a failure or loss, if the originals are destroyed or out of service.

Bandwidth: The range between the highest and lowest transmittable frequencies.

Bar Code: A printed machine-readable code that consists of parallel bars of varied width and spacing.

Base Case: System Evaluation. A standardized body of data is created for testing purposes. The data is normally established by the users. Base case validates production application systems and tests the ongoing accurate operation of the system.

Baseboard: A form of modulation in which data signals are pulsed directly on the transmission medium without frequency division and usually utilizes a transceiver. In baseband the entire bandwidth of the transmission medium (e.g. coaxial cable) is utilized for a single channel. Contrasts with Broadband.

Batch Control: Correctness checks built into data processing systems and applied to batches of input data, particularly in the data preparation stage. There are two main forms of batch controls: Sequence Control, which involves numbering the records in a batch consecutively so that the presence of each record can be confirmed and Control Totals which involve establishing record counts, or totals of the values in selected fields within each record and checking these totals. Batch Control manually groups input transactions in order to provide control totals.

Batch Processing: The processing of a group of transactions at one time. Transactions are collected and processed against the master files at a specified time.

Baud Rate: The rate of transmission for telecommunication data; expressed in bits per second (bps).

Benchmark: A test that has been designed to evaluate the performance of a system. In a benchmark test, a system is subjected to a known workload, and the performance of the system against this workload is measured. Typically, the purpose is to compare the measured performance with that of other systems that have been subject to the same benchmark test.

Binary Code: A code whose representation is limited to 0 and 1.

Biometrics: An interface technique that verifies an individual's identity by analyzing a unique, inborn, physical attribute. These attributes are usually identified by retinal scans, voice analyzers, or palm scans.

Biometric Locks: Door and entry locks that are activated by such biometric features as voice, eye retina, fingerprint, or signature.

Bridge: Device which connects two similar networks together.

Broadband: In broadband, multiple channels are formed by dividing the transmission medium into discrete frequency segments and generally make use of a modem. Contrasts with Baseband.

Buffer: Memory reserved to hold data temporarily. Buffers are used to offset differences between operating speeds of different devices, e.g. a printer and a high speed computer. In a program, buffers are reserved areas of RAM that hold data while it is being processed.

BUS: Common path or channel between hardware devices. It can be between components internal to a computer or external between computers in a communications network,

Bus Topology: A type of Local Area Network (LAN) architecture in which each station is directly attached to a common communication channel. Signals transmitted over the channel take the form of messages. As each message passes along the channel, each station receives it. Each station then determines, based on an address contained in the message, whether to accept and process the message or simply to ignore it.

Business Impact Analysis (BIA): Process to determine the impact of losing the support of any resource. The business impact analysis assessment study will establish the escalation of that loss over time. It is predicated on the fact that senior management, when provided reliable data to document the potential impact of a lost resource, can make the appropriate decision.

Business Process Re-engineering (BPR): Modern expression for Organizational Development stemming from IS/IT impacts. The ultimate goal of BPR is to yield a better performing structure, more responsive to the customer base and market conditions, while yielding material cost savings. To reengineer means redesigning a structure and procedures with intelligence and skills, and be well informed about all of the attendant factors of a given situation. To obtain the maximum benefits from mechanization as a basic rationale.

Business Risk: Risks that could impact the organization's ability to perform business or provide a service. They can be financial, regulatory, or control-oriented.

Bypass Label Processing (BLP): A technique of reading a computer file while bypassing the internal file/data set label. This process could result in bypassing the security access control system.

Card Swipes: A physical control technique that uses a secured card or ID to gain access to a highly sensitive location. Card swipes, if built correctly, act as a preventative control in gaining physical access to those sensitive locations. After a card has been swiped, the application that is attached to the physical card swipe device logs all card users that try to access the secured location. The card swipe device prevents unauthorized access and logs all attempts to access the secured location.

Computer Aided Software Engineering (CASE): The use of software packages that aid in the development of all phases of an information system. System analysis, design, programming, and documentation are provided. Changes introduced in one CASE chart will automatically update all other related charts. CASE can be installed on a microcomputer for easy access.

Central Processing Unit (CPU): Computer hardware which houses the electronic circuits that control/direct all operations in the computer system.

Centralized Data Processing: Identified by one central processor and databases that form a distributed processing configuration.

Challenge/Response Token: A method of user authentication. The user enters an ID and password and, in return, is issued a challenge by the system. The system compares the user's response against the challenge of the computed response. If the responses match, the user is allowed access to the system. The system issues a different challenge each time. In effect, it requires a new password for each logon.

Check Digit: A numeric value that has been calculated mathematically is added to data to ensure that original data has not been altered or that an incorrect but valid match has occurred. This control is effective in detecting transposition and transcription errors.

Check Digit Verification (self-checking digit): A programmed edit check where an extra digit is included to a piece of data like a customer number, vendor number, or part number. Using a routine the computer checks the validity of the incoming data.

Checkpoint Restart Procedures: A point in a routine at which sufficient information can be stored to permit restarting the computation from that point.

Ciphertext: Digital information generated by the encryption in order to protect the cleartext. The ciphertext is unintelligible to the reader.

Circuit-Switched Network: Circuit-switched network is a data transmission service requiring the establishment of a circuit-switched connection before data can be transferred from source data terminal equipment (DTE) to a sink DTE. Note: a circuit-switched data transmission service uses a connection-oriented network.

Circular Routing: In open systems architecture, circular routing is the logical path of a message in a communications network based on a series of gates at the physical network layer in the Open Systems Interconnection (OSI).

Client/Server: A group of computers connected by a communications network where the client is the requesting machine and the server is the supplying machine. Software is specialized at both ends. Processing may take place at either the client or the server, but that is transparent to the user.

Cluster Controller: A communications terminal control hardware unit that controls a number of computer terminals. All messages are buffered by the controller and then transmitted to the receiver.

Coaxial Cable: An insulated wire that runs through the middle of each cable. A second wire surrounds the insulation of the inner wire like a sheath. The outer insulation wraps the second wire. Coaxial cable has a greater transmission capacity than standard twisted pair cables but has a limited range of effective distance.

Cold Site: An IS backup facility that has the necessary electrical and physical components of a computer facility but does not have the computer equipment in place. The site is ready to receive the necessary replacement computer equipment in the event the user has to move from their main computing location to the alternative computer facility.

Communications Controller: Small computers used to connect and coordinate communication links between distributed or remote devices and the main computer, thus freeing the main computer from this overhead function.

Comparison Program: A program for the examination of data by using logical or conditional tests to determine, or to identify, similarities or differences.

Compensating Control: An internal control which reduces the risk of an existing or potential control weakness resulting in errors and omissions.

Compiler: A software program that translates programming language into machine language which a computer understands. A compiler usually generates assembly language first. The assembly language is then converted to machine language.

Completeness Check: A procedure designed to ensure that no fields are missing from the record and that the entire record has been checked.

Compliance Testing: Audit tests which determine if internal controls are being applied in a manner described in the documentation and in accordance with the management's intent.

Comprehensive Audit: An audit designed to determine the accuracy of financial records, as well as evaluate the internal controls of a function or department.

Computer Assisted Audit Tools and Techniques (CAATT): Any automated audit tool or technique, such as generalized audit software, test data generators, computerized audit programs, and specialized audit utilities.

Computer Sequence Checking: Verifies that the control number follows sequentially, and any control numbers out of sequence are rejected or noted on an exception report for further research.

Console Log: An automated detail report of computer system activity.

Continuous Auditing Approach: This approach allows IS auditors to monitor system reliability on a continuous basis and to gather selective audit evidence through the computer.

Control Group: Members of the operations area that are responsible for the collection, logging, and submission of input for the various user groups.

Control Risk: The risk that a material misstatement, which could occur in an assertion, will not be prevented or detected on a timely basis by an entity's internal controls structure.

Control Section: The area of the central processing unit that executes software, allocates internal memory, and transfers operations between the arithmetic-logic, internal storage, and output sections of the computer.

Corrective Controls: These controls are designed to correct errors, omissions, and unauthorized uses and intrusions once they are detected.

Critical Path Method (CPM): A project management planning and control tool. The critical path is a series of activities and tasks in the project that have no built-in slack time. Any task in the critical path that takes longer than expected will lengthen the total time of the project.

Cathode Ray Tube (CRT): A vacuum tube which displays data by means of an electron beam striking the screen, which is coated with suitable phosphor material, or a device similar to a television screen upon which data can be displayed.

Database: A stored collection of related data needed by organizations and individuals to meet their information processing and retrieval requirements.

Database Administrator (DBA): An individual or department responsible for the security and information classification of the shared data stored on a database system. This responsibility includes the design, definition, and maintenance of the database.

Database Management System (DBMS): A complex set of software programs that controls the organization, storage, and retrieval of data in a database. It also controls the security and integrity of the database.

Database Replication: The process of creating and managing duplicate versions of a database. Replication not only copies a database but also synchronizes a set of replicas so that changes made to one replica are reflected in all the others. The beauty of replication is that it enables many users to work with their own local copy of a database but have the database updated as if they were working on a single centralized database. For database applications where users are geographically widely distributed, replication is often the most efficient method of database access.

Database Specifications: These are the requirements for establishing a database application. They include field definitions, field requirements, and reporting requirements for the individual information in the database.

Data Communications: The transfer of data between distant computer sites devices using telephone lines, microwave, and/or satellite links.

Data Custodian: Individuals and departments responsible for the storage and safeguarding of computerized information. This typically is the IS group.

Data Dictionary: A data dictionary is a database which contains the name, type, range of values, source, and authorization for access for each data element in a database. It also indicates which application programs use that data so that when a data structure change is contemplated, a list of the affected programs can be generated. The data dictionary may be a stand-alone information system used for management or documentation purposes or it may control the operation of a database.

Data Diddling: Changing data for malicious intents before or during input into the system.

Data Encryption Standard (DES): A private cryptosystem that is a standard encryption technique published by the National Bureau of Standards (NBS) as a predecessor of the National Institute of Standards and Technology (NIST), USA. The DES has been commonly used for data encryption in the forms of software and hardware implementation. The strength of the DES depends on the number of encryption key bits, e.g. 56 bits. On the basis of the 56 bits encryption key, the DES performs the 16 round iterations of encryption process repeatedly. The encryption process consists of the substitutions, the permutations, and the mathematical XOR (Exclusive-OR) operations (also see encryption).

Data Leakage: Siphoning out or leaking information by dumping computer files or stealing computer reports and tapes.

Data-Oriented Systems Development: The purpose is to provide usable data rather than a function. The focus of the development is to provide ad hoc reporting for users by developing a suitable accessible database of information, rather than simply addressing a given limited process development.

Data Owner: Individuals, normally managers or directors, who have responsibility for the accurate reporting and use of the computerized data.

Data Security: Those controls which protect information, both computerized and hard copy, from accidental or intentional unauthorized addition, deletion, disclosure, modification, or destruction.

Data Structure: The relationships among files in a database and among data items within each file.

Decentralization: The process of distributing computer processing to different locations within an organization.

Decision Support Systems (DSS): An interactive system that provides the user with easy access to decision models and data in order to support semi-structured decision-making tasks.

Decryption: A technique used to recover the original plaintext from the ciphertext such that it is intelligible to the reader. The decryption is a reverse process of the encryption.

Decryption Key: A piece of information, as a digitized form, used to recover the plaintext from the corresponding ciphertext by decryption.

Demodulation: The process of converting an analog telecommunications signal into a digital computer signal.

Detection Risk: The risk that material errors or misstatements that have occurred will not be detected by the auditor.

Detective Control: These controls exist to detect and report when errors, omissions, and unauthorized use or entry occur.

Dial-Back: Used as a control over dial-up telecommunications lines. The telecommunications link established through dial-up into the computer from a remote location is interrupted so the computer can dial back to the caller. The link is permitted only if the caller is from a valid phone number or telecommunications channel.

Dial-In Access Controls: Controls that prevent unauthorized access from remote users that attempt to access a secured environment. These controls range from dial-back controls to remote user authentication.

Digital Signature: A piece of information, as a digitized form of signature, used to authenticate the signer who already signed the message by his (or her) secret key. The digital signature regarding the message can be obtained by the decryption of the public key cryptosystems.

Diskless Workstations: A workstation or PC on a network that does not have its own disk. Instead, it stores files on a network file server or on the cloud.

Distributed Data Processing Network: A system of computers connected by a communications network. Each computer processes its data, and the network supports the system as a whole. Such a network enhances communication among the linked computers and allows access to shared files.

Downloading: The act of transferring computerized information from one computer to another computer.

Down Time Report: A report that identifies the elapsed time when a computer is not operating correctly because of machine failure.

Dry-Pipe Fire Extinguisher System: Refers to a sprinkler system that does not have water in the pipes during idle usage, unlike a fully charged fire extinguisher system that has water in the pipes at all times. The dry-pipe system is activated at the time of the fire alarm and water is emitted to the pipes from a water reservoir for discharge to the location under fire.

Dumb Terminal: A display terminal without processing capability. Dumb terminals are dependent upon the main computer for processing. All entered data is accepted without further editing or validation.

Duplex Routing: The method or communication mode of routing data over the communication network (also see Half Duplex and Full Duplex).

Echo Checks: Detects line errors by re-transmitting data back to the sending device for comparison with the original transmission.

Edit Controls: Detect errors in the input portion of information that is sent to the computer for processing. The controls may be manual or automated and allow the user to edit data errors before processing.

Editing: Editing ensures that data conforms to predetermined criteria and enables early identification of potential errors.

Electronic Cash: An electronic form functionally equivalent to cash in order to make and receive payments in cyberbanking.

Electronic Data Interchange (EDI): Electronic data interchange is the electronic transmission of documents in a machine-readable form between two organizations. EDI promotes a more efficient paperless environment. EDI transmissions can replace the use of standard documents, including invoices or purchase orders.

Electronic Funds Transfer (EFT): Electronic funds transfer is the exchange of money via telecommunications. EFT refers to any financial transaction that originates at a terminal and transfers a sum of money from one account to another.

Email: Interpersonal messaging – an individual using a terminal, PC, or an application can access a network to send an unstructured message to another individual or group of people. X.400 has become the standard governing the exchange of electronic mail between services most commonly in Europe and Canada as an alternative to SMTP.

Embedded Audit Modules: An embedded audit module is a screening process which is incorporated into the regular production programs. The module selects items during the regular production runs that fulfill certain criteria established by the auditor, and usually outputs or copies these items to a file or report.

Encryption: A technique used to protect the plaintext by coding the data such that it is unintelligible to the reader.

Encapsulation (objects): Encapsulation is the technique used by layered protocols in which a lower layer protocol accepts a message from a higher layer protocol and places it in the data portion of a frame in the lower layer.

Encryption Key: A piece of information, as a digitized form, used to convert the plaintext to the ciphertext by encryption.

End-User Computing: The ability of the end-user to design and implement their own information system, utilizing computer software products.

Ethernet: Since the 1990s Ethernet has been a popular network protocol and cabling scheme that uses a bus topology and Carrier Sense Multiple Access/Collision Detection (CSMA/CD) to prevent network failures or collisions when two devices try to access the network at the same time.

Exception Reports: An exception report is generated by a program which identifies transactions or data which appear to be incorrect. These items may be outside a predetermined range, or may not conform to specified criteria.

Executable Code: Computer code that has been converted from high level syntax or source code by a compiler into machine code. This module is sometimes referred to as 'object' code or 'load' member by different manufacturers or operating environments.

Expert Systems: Expert systems are the most prevalent type of computer systems which arise from the research of artificial intelligence. An expert system has a built-in hierarchy of rules which are acquired from human experts in the appropriate field. Once input is provided the system should be able to define the nature of the problem and provide recommendations to solve the problem.

Exposure: Potential adverse result or consequence to be considered in evaluation of internal controls. Strengthening internal controls can reduce exposure but seldom eliminate it.

Extended Binary-Coded Decimal Interchange Code (EBCDIC): An 8-bit code representing 256 characters. Used in many large computer systems.

Feasibility Study: A phase of the SDLC methodology that researches the feasibility and adequacy of resources for the development or acquisition of a system solution to a user need.

Fiber Optic Cable: Glass fibers that transmit binary signals over a telecommunications network. Fiber optic systems have low transmission losses as compared to the twisted pairs cable. They do not radiate energy or conduct electricity. They are free from corruption and lightning-induced interference and reduce the risk of wiretaps.

Field: An individual data element in a computer file. Examples include Employee Name, Customer Address, Account Number, Product, Unit Price, and Product Quantity in Stock.

File: A named collection of related records. In relational databases, referred to as a Table.

File Layout: Specifies the length of the file's record and the sequence and size of its fields. A file layout will also specify the type of data contained within each field. For example, alphanumeric, zoned decimal, packed, and binary are types of data.

File Server: A high capacity disk storage device or a computer that stores data centrally for network users and manages access to that data. File servers can be dedicated so that no process other than network management can be executed while the network is available. File servers can be non-dedicated so that standard user applications can run while the network is available.

Financial Audit: An audit designed to determine the accuracy of financial records and information.

Firmware: Memory chips that hold their content when power is turned off.

Firewalls: Devices that form a barrier between a secure and an open environment. Usually, the open environment is considered hostile. The most notable environment that is hostile is the internet. In other words, a Firewall acts as a system or combination of systems that enforces a boundary between two or more networks.

Format Checking: The application of an edit using a predefined field definition to a submitted information stream. A test for conformance of data to a predefined format.

Fourth Generation Language: English-like, user friendly, non-procedural computer languages used to program and/or read and process computer files.

Frame-Relay: A packet-switched wide area network technology that provides faster performance than older packet-switched WAN technologies such as X.25 networks, because it was designed for today's reliable circuits and performs less rigorous error detection. Frame relay is best suited for data and image transfers. Because of its variable-length packet architecture, it is not the most efficient technology for real-time voice and video. In a frame relay network, end nodes establish a connection via a Permanent Virtual Circuit (PVC).

Fraud Risk: The risk that activities will include deliberate circumvention of controls with the intent to conceal the perpetuation of irregularities. The unauthorized use of assets or services and abetting or helping to conceal.

Full Duplex: A communications channel over which data can be simultaneously sent and received.

Function Point Analysis: A technique used to determine the size of a development task, based on the number of function points. Function points are factors such as inputs, outputs, inquiries, logical internal sites, etc.

GANTT Chart: A bar chart plotting the phases or activities of a project against a predefined timeline to completion.

Gateway: A hardware/software package which is used to interconnect networks with different protocols. The gateway has its own processor and memory and can perform protocol and bandwidth conversions.

General Computer Controls: Basic broad areas of control that protect against most broad risks. These are high level risks not application-specific. Normally these include organizational, security, general operations, and disaster recovery.

Generalized Audit Software (GAS): Multi-purpose audit software which can be used for such general processes as record selection, matching, recalculation, data analytics, and reporting.

Hacker: An individual who maliciously attempts to gain unauthorized access to a computer system.

Half Duplex: A communications channel which can handle only one-directional signal at a time. The two stations must alternate their transmissions.

Handprint Scanner: Biometric controls that are used to authenticate a user through palm scans.

Hardware: Relates to the technical and physical features of the computer.

Hash Total: The total of any numeric data field on a document or computer file. This total is then checked against a control total of the same field to facilitate accuracy of processing.

Hexadecimal: A numbering system that uses a base of 16 and requires 16 digits: 0, 1, 2, 3, 4, 5, 6, 7, 8, 9, A, B, C, D, E, and F. Programmers use hexadecimal numbers as a convenient way of representing binary numbers.

Hierarchical Database: A database structured in a tree/root or parent/child relationship. Each parent can have many children, but each child may have only one parent.

Hotsite: A fully operational off-site data processing facility equipped with both hardware and system software to be used in the event of a disaster.

Image Processing: The process of electronically inputting source documents by taking an image of the document, eliminating the need for key entry.

Indexed Sequential Access Method (ISAM): A disk access method that stores data sequentially while maintaining an index of key fields to all the records in the file for direct access capability. The sequential order of the file would be the one most commonly used for batch processing and printing.

Indexed Sequential File: A file format in which records are organized and can be accessed according to a pre-established key that is part of the record.

Information Engineering: Data-oriented development techniques that work on the premise that data is at the center of information processing and that certain data relationships are significant to a business and must be represented in the data structure of its systems.

Information Processing Facility (IPF): The computer room and support areas.

Inherent Risk: The risk that a material error could occur, assuming that there are no related internal controls to prevent or detect the error. Also see Control Risk.

Inheritance (objects): Inheritance (objects) refer to database structures that have a strict hierarchy (no multiple inheritance), Inheritance (objects) can initiate other objects irrespective of the class hierarchy, thus there is no strict hierarchy of objects.

Initial Program Load (IPL): The initialization procedure that causes an operating system to be loaded into storage at the beginning of a workday or after a system malfunction.

Input Controls: Techniques and procedures used to verify, validate, and edit data to ensure that only correct data is entered into the computer.

Integrated Service Digital Network (ISDN): A public end-to-end digital telecommunications network with signaling, switching, and transport capabilities supporting a wide range of services accessed by standardized interfaces with integrated customer control.

Integrated Test Facilities (ITF): Test data is processed in production systems. The data usually represents a set of fictitious entities such as departments, customers, and products. Output reports are verified to confirm the correctness of the processing.

Intelligent Terminal: A terminal with built-in processing capability. It has no disk or tape storage, but has memory. It interacts with the user by editing and validating data as it is entered prior to final processing.

Interface Testing: A testing technique that is used to evaluate outputs from one application as the information is sent as inputs to another application.

Internal Storage: The main memory of the computer's central processing unit.

Internet: Two or more networks connected by a router. The world's largest network using TCP/IP protocols to link government, university, and commercial institutions.

Internet Packet (IP) Spoofing: An attack using packets with the spoofed source Internet Packet (IP) addresses. This technique exploits applications that use authentication based on IP addresses. This technique also leads unauthorized user possibility to take the root access on the target system.

Irregularities: Intentional violations of established policy or willful misstatements or omissions of information.

Job Control Language (JCL): A programming language used to control run routines in connection with performing tasks on a computer.

Leased Lines: A line permanently assigned to connect two points, as opposed to a dial up line which is only available and open when a connection is made by dialing the target machine or network. Also known as a dedicated line.

Librarian: The individual responsible for the safeguarding and maintenance of all program and data files.

Limit Check: Tests of specified amount fields against stipulated high or low limits of acceptability. When both high and low values are used, the test may be called a 'range check'.

Link Editor (Linkage Editor): A utility program that combines several separately compiled modules into one, resolving internal references between them.

Local Area Network (LAN): Communications networks that serve several users within a specified geographical area. Personal computer LANs function as distributed processing systems in which each computer in the network does its own processing and manages some of its data. Shared data is stored in a file server which acts as a remote disk drive to all users in the network.

Log: To record details of information or events in an organized record-keeping system, usually sequenced in the order they occurred.

Logical Access Controls: The policies, procedures, organizational structure, and electronic access controls designed to restrict access to computer software and data files.

Logoff: Disconnecting from the computer.

Logon: The act of connecting to the computer. Typically requires entry of a user ID and password into a computer terminal.

Machine Language: The logic language a computer understands.

Magnetic Card Reader: A card reader that reads cards with a magnetic surface on which data can be stored and retrieved.

Magnetic Ink Character Recognition (MICR): Used to electronically input, read, and interpret information directly from a source document. Requires the source document to have specially coded magnetic ink typeset (commonly E13B).

Management Information system (MIS): An organized assembly of resources and procedures required to collect, process, and distribute data for use in decision making.

Mapping: Diagramming data that is to be exchanged electronically, including how it is to be used and what business management systems need it. Preliminary step for developing an applications link. Performed by the functional manager responsible for a business management system.

Masking: A computerized technique of blocking out the display of sensitive information, such as passwords on a computer terminal or report.

Master File: A file of semi-permanent information that is used frequently for processing data or for more than one purpose.

Materiality: An auditing concept regarding the importance of an item of information with regard to its impact or effect on the functioning of the entity being audited.

Memory Dump: The act of copying raw data from one place to another with little or no formatting for readability. Usually, dump refers to copying data from main memory to a display screen or a printer. Dumps are useful for diagnosing bugs. After a program fails, the dump can be studied and analyzed for the contents of memory at the time of the failure. Dumps are usually output in a difficult-to-read form (that is, binary, octal, or hexadecimal), so a memory dump will not help you unless you know exactly what to look for.

Message Switching: A telecommunications traffic-controlling methodology in which a complete message is sent to a concentration point and stored until the communications path is established.

Microwave Transmission: A high-capacity line-of-sight transmission of data signals through the atmosphere often requiring relay stations.

Middleware: Another term for an Application Programmer Interface (API). It refers to the interfaces that allow programmers to access lower or higher level services by providing an intermediary layer that includes function calls to the services.

Modem (Modulator-Demodulator): Adapts a terminal or computer to a communications network. Modems turn digital pulses from the computer into frequencies within the audio range of the telephone system. When acting in the receiver capacity, a modem decodes incoming frequencies.

Modulation: The process of converting a digital computer signal into an analog telecommunications signal.

Multiplexer: A device used for combining several lower speed channels into a higher speed channel.

Multiplexing: Transmission of more than one signal across a physical channel.

Network: A system of interconnected computers and the communications equipment used to connect them.

Network Administrator: The person responsible for maintaining a LAN and assisting end-users.

Node: A major point at which terminals are given access to a network.

Noise: Disturbances in data transmissions which cause messages to be misinterpreted by the receiver, e.g. static.

Normalization: Elimination of redundant data.

Numeric Check: An edit check designed to ensure the data in a particular field is numeric.

Object Code: The output from a compiler which translates high-level languages into machine code.

Offline Files: Computer file storage media not physically connected to the computer. This may be optical disk, tape, or tape cartridge, and is generally used for back-up purposes.

Offsite Storage: A storage facility located away from the building housing the primary IPF, used for storage of computer media such as offline backup data and storage files.

Online Data Processing: Processing is achieved by entering information into the computer via a terminal. The computer immediately accepts or rejects the information as it is entered.

Open Systems: Systems for which detailed specifications for the components and their composition are published in a non-proprietary environment, thereby enabling competing organizations to use these standard components to build competitive systems. The advantages of using open systems include portability, inter-operability, and integration.

Operating System: A master control program that runs the computer and acts as a scheduler and traffic controller. It is the first program copied into the computer's memory after the computer is turned on, and must reside in memory at all times. It sets the standards for the application programs that run in it.

Operational Audit: An audit designed to evaluate the various internal controls, economy, efficiency, and effectiveness of a function or department.

Operational Control: These controls deal with the everyday operation of a company or organization to ensure all objectives are achieved.

Operator Console: A special terminal used by computer operations personnel to control computer and systems operations functions. These terminals typically provide a high level of computer access, and should be properly secured.

Optical Character Recognition: Used to electronically scan and input written information from a source document.

Optical Scanner: An input device that reads characters and images that are printed or painted on a paper form into the computer (see Image Processing).

Output Analyzer: Checks the accuracy of the results produced by a test run. There are three types of checks that an output analyzer can perform. First, if a standard set of test data and test results exists for a program, the output of a test run after program maintenance can be compared with the set of results that should be produced. Second, as programmers prepare test data and calculate the expected results, these results can be stored on a file and the output analyzer compares the actual results of a test run with the expected results. Third, the output analyzer can act as a query language; it accepts queries about whether certain relationships exist in the file of output results and reports compliance or non-compliance.

Packet: A block of data for data transmission. A packet contains both routing information and data.

Packet Switching: The process of transmitting messages in convenient pieces that can be reassembled at the destination.

Parallel Simulation: Parallel simulation involves the auditor writing a program to replicate those application processes that are critical to an audit opinion and using this program to reprocess application system data. The results produced are compared with the results produced by the application system and any discrepancies identified.

Parity Check: A general hardware control which helps to detect data errors when data is read from memory or communicated from one computer to another. A one-bit digit (either 0 or 1) is added to a data item to indicate whether the sum of that data item's bit is odd or even. When the parity bit disagrees with the sum of the other bits, the computer reports an error. The probability of a parity check detecting an error is 50 percent.

Partitioned File: A file format in which the file is divided into multiple sub-files, and a directory is established to locate each sub-file.

Passive Assault: In a Passive Assault, intruders attempt to learn some characteristic of the data being transmitted. They may be able to read the contents of the data so the privacy of the data is violated. Alternatively, although the content of the data itself may remain secure, intruders may read and analyze the clear-text source and destination identifiers attached to a message for routing purposes, or they may examine the lengths and frequency of messages being transmitted.

Password: A protected, generally computer-encrypted string of characters that authenticate a computer user to the computer system.

Peripherals: Auxiliary computer hardware equipment used for input, output, and data storage. Examples include disk drives and printers.

Piggy-Backing: Following an authorized person into a restricted access area. Electronically attaching to an authorized tele-communications link to intercept transmissions.

PIN (Personal Identification Number): A type of password; that is, a secret number assigned to an individual which, in conjunction with some means of identifying the individual, serves to verify the authenticity of the individual. PINs have been adopted by financial institutions as the primary means of verifying customers in an electronic funds transfer system (EFTS).

Plaintext: Digital information that is intelligible to the reader (i.e. clear text).

Polymorphism (objects): Polymorphism refers to database structures that send the same command to different child objects which can produce different results, depending on their family hierarchical tree structures.

Point of Sale Systems (POS): Point of sale systems enable the capture of data at the time and place of transaction. POS terminals may include use of optical scanners for use with bar codes or magnetic card readers for use with credit cards. POS systems may be online to a central computer or may use stand-alone terminals or microcomputers that hold the transactions until the end of a specified period when they are sent to the main computer for batch processing.

Port: An interface point between the CPU and a peripheral device.

Posting: The process of actually entering transactions into computerized or manual files. Such transactions might immediately update the master files or may result in memo posting, in which the transactions are accumulated over a period of time, then applied to master file updating.

Preventive Controls: These controls are designed to prevent or restrict an error, omission, or unauthorized intrusion.

Private Key Cryptosystems: Used in data encryption, it uses a secret key to encrypt the plaintext to the ciphertext. It also uses the same key to decrypt the ciphertext to the corresponding plaintext. In this case, the key is symmetric such that the encryption key is equivalent to the decryption key.

Production Programs: Programs that are used to process 'live' or actual data that was received as inputs into the production environment.

Production Software: Software that is being used and executed to support normal and authorized organizational operations. Such software is to be distinguished from 'test' software which is being developed or modified, but has not yet been authorized for live use by management.

Program Evaluation Review Technique (PERT): A project management technique used in the planning and control of system projects.

Program Flowcharts: Program flowcharts show the sequence of instructions in a single program or subroutine, symbols used should be the internationally accepted standard. Program flowcharts should be updated when necessary.

Program Narratives: Program narratives provide a detailed explanation of program flowcharts including control points and any external input.

Program Object Code: Machine instructions produced from a compiler or assembler program that has accepted and translated the source code into machine readable instructions.

Project Management: An automated or manual method for reviewing and controlling an audit or project. Examples include GANTT charts and PERT charts, which highlight and monitor progress and project milestones.

Protocol: Rules by which a network operates and controls the flow and priority of transmissions.

Protocol Converter: Hardware devices that convert between asynchronous and synchronous transmissions.

Prototyping: A system development technique that enables users and developers to reach agreement on system requirements.

Prototyping uses programmed simulation techniques to represent a model of the final system to the user for advisement and critique. The emphasis is on end-user screens and reports. Internal controls are not a priority item since this is only a model.

Proxy Server: A server that acts on behalf of a user. Typical proxies accept a connection from a user and make a decision as to whether or not the user or client IP address is permitted to use the proxy. Perhaps the proxy will do additional authentication, and then complete a connection on behalf of the user to a remote destination.

Public Key Cryptosystems: Used in data encryption, it uses an encryption key as a public key to encrypt the plaintext to the ciphertext. It uses a different decryption key as a secret key to decrypt the ciphertext to the corresponding plaintext. In contrast to the private key cryptosystems, the decryption key should be secret, however, the encryption key can be known to everyone. In the public key cryptosystems, two keys are asymmetric such that the encryption key is not equivalent to the decryption key.

Queue: A group of items which are waiting to be serviced or processed.

Random Access Memory (RAM): The computer's primary working memory. Each byte of memory can be accessed randomly regardless of adjacent bytes.

Range Check: Range checks ensure that data falls within a predetermined range (also see limit checks).

Real-Time Processing: An interactive online system capability that immediately updates computer files when transactions are initiated through a terminal.

Reasonableness Check: Reasonableness checks compare data to predefined reasonability limits or occurrence rates established for the data.

Reciprocal Agreement: Emergency processing agreements between two or more organizations with similar equipment or applications. Typically, participants promise to provide processing time to each other when an emergency arises.

Record: A collection of related information treated as a unit. Separate fields within the record are used for processing of the information. Also, a **Tuple** in Relational Databases.

Record, Screen, and Report Layouts: Record layouts provide information regarding the type of record, its size, and the type of data contained in the record. Screen and report layouts describe what information is provided and necessary for input.

Redundancy Check: Detects transmission errors by appending calculated bits onto the end of each segment of data.

Re-engineering: A process involving the extraction of components from existing systems and restructuring these components to develop new systems or to enhance the efficiency of existing systems. Existing software systems thus can be modernized to prolong their functionality. An example of this is a software code translator that can take an existing hierarchical database system and transpose it to a relational database system. CASE includes a source code re-engineering feature.

Regression Testing: A testing technique used to retest earlier program amends or logical errors that occurred during the initial testing phase.

Remote Job Entry (RJE): The transmission of Job Control Language (JCL) and batches of transactions from a remote terminal location.

Repository: The central database that stores and organizes data.

Request for Proposal (RFP): A document distributed to software vendors requesting them to submit a proposal to develop or provide a software product.

Requirements Definition: A phase of the SDLC methodology where the affected user groups define the requirements of the system for meeting the defined needs.

Reverse Engineering: A software engineering technique whereby existing application system code can be redesigned and coded using CASE technology.

Ring Topology: A type of LAN architecture in which the cable forms a loop with stations attached at intervals around the loop. Signals transmitted around the ring take the form of messages. The messages are received by each station and each station determines, on the basis of an address, whether to accept or process a given message. However, after receiving a message, each station acts as a repeater, re-transmitting the message at its original signal strength.

Risk: The probability of occurrence of an adverse event or action.

Rounding Down: A method of computer fraud involving a computer code that instructs the computer to remove small amounts of money from an authorized computer transaction by rounding down to the nearest whole value denomination and rerouting the rounded off amount to the perpetrator's account. Also referred to as a **Salami Technique.**

Router: A networking device that can send (route) packets to the connected LAN segment, based on addressing at the Network Layer (Layer 3) in the OSI model. Networks connected by routers can use different or similar networking protocols. Routers usually are capable of filtering packets based on parameters, such as source address, destination address, protocol, and network application (ports).

RS-232 Interface: Interface between data terminal equipment and data communications equipment employing serial binary data interchange.

RSA: A public key cryptosystem developed by R. Rivest, A. Shamir, and L. Adleman. The RSA has two different keys: the public encryption key and the secret decryption key. The strength of the RSA depends on the difficulty of the prime number factorization. For the applications with high level security, the number of the decryption key bits is generally greater than 512 bits. The RSA provides both the encryption and the digital signature.

Run Instructions: Computer operating instructions which detail the step-by-step processes that are to occur so an application system can be properly executed. Also identifies how to address problems that occur during processing.

Run-to-Run Totals: Run-to-run totals provide verification that all transmitted data is read and processed.

Salami Technique: A method of computer fraud that involves computer code that instructs the computer to 'slice off' small amounts of money from an authorized computer transaction, and reroute this amount to the perpetrator's account.

Scheduling: A method used in the Information Processing Facility to determine and establish the sequence of computer job processing.

Screening Routers: A router configured to permit or deny traffic based on a set of permission rules installed by the administrator.

Systems Development Life Cycle (SDLC): The phases of the development deployed in the development or acquisition of a software system. Typical phases include the feasibility study, requirements study, requirements definition, detailed design, programming, testing, implementation, and post-implementation review.

Security Administrator: The person responsible for implementing, monitoring, and enforcing security rules established and authorized by management.

Security Software: Software used to administer logical security. Usually includes authentication of users, access granting according to predefined rules, monitoring, and reporting functions.

Segregation of Duties: Distributing work responsibilities such that individuals are prevented from having responsibility for entry, edit, and review of a transaction or function. This is the primary control to prevent accidental or purposeful errors, omissions, or misuse of company assets.

Sequence Check: Verifies that the control number follows sequentially, and any control numbers out of sequence are rejected or noted on an exception report for further research (can be alpha or numeric and usually utilizes a 'key' field).

Sequential File: A computer file storage format in which one record follows another. Records can be accessed sequentially only. Required with magnetic tape.

Service Bureau: A computer facility which provides data processing services to clients on a continual basis.

Smart Card: With see-through security, this process eliminates the need for traditional logon-ID password security. The person logging onto the system uses a personal hand-held device which contains an algorithm used for one-time passwords. The user logs on through telecommunications lines in which a random encrypted password is sent by the computer to the hand-held device. The hand-held device decrypts the password and the password is then re-entered by the user into the device which sends it back to the computer for validation and system entry. The one-time passwords must match to gain entry into the system.

Sniffing: An attack capturing sensitive pieces of information, e.g. passwords, passing through the network.

Software: Programs and systems which enable and facilitate use of the computer. Software controls the operation of the hardware.

Source Code: Source code is the language in which a program is written. Source code is translated into object code by assemblers and compilers. In some cases, source code may be automatically converted into another language by a conversion program. Source code is not executable by the computer directly. It must first be converted into machine language.

Source Code Compare Programs: Programs that provide assurance that the software being audited is the correct version of the software by providing a meaningful listing of any discrepancies between the two versions of the program.

Source Documents: The forms used to record data that has been captured. A source document may be a piece of paper, a turnaround document, or an image displayed for online data input.

Split Data Systems: A condition in which each of an organization's regional locations maintains its own financial and operational data while sharing processing with an organization-wide, centralized database. This permits easy sharing of data while maintaining a certain level of autonomy.

Spool (Simultaneous Peripheral Operations Online): An automated function in which electronic data being transmitted between storage areas is 'spooled' or stored until the receiving device or storage area is prepared and able to receive the information. This operation allows more efficient electronic data transfers from one device to another by permitting higher speed sending functions, such as internal memory, to continue with other operations instead of waiting on the slower speed receiving device, such as printers.

Standing Data: Permanent reference data used in transaction processing. This data is changed infrequently, such as a product price file or a name and address file.

Star Topology: A type of LAN architecture that utilizes a central controller to which all nodes are directly connected. All transmissions from one station to another pass through the central controller, which is responsible for managing and controlling all communication. The central controller often acts as a switching device.

Structured Programming: Top-down technique of designing programs and systems. Makes programs more readable, more reliable, and more easily maintained.

Structured Query Language (SQL): The primary language used by both application programmers and end-users in accessing relational databases.

Substantive Testing: A method of audit testing to assure that there are adequate internal controls in place. Substantive testing will be limited when there is a low risk of control failure. Conversely, if the testing of controls reveals weaknesses in control, substantive testing would be performed.

Surge Suppressor: Filters out electrical surges and spikes.

Symmetric Key Encryption: Two trading partners both share one or more secrets. No one else can read their messages. A different key (or set of keys) is needed for each pair of trading partners. Same key is used for encryption and decryption.

Synchronous Transmission: Block-at-a-time data transmission.

Systems Analysis: The systems development phase in which systems specifications and conceptual designs are developed, based on end-user needs and requirements.

System Exit: Special system software features and utilities that allow the user to perform complex system maintenance. Use of these exits often permit the user to operate outside of the security access control system.

System Flowcharts: System flowcharts are graphical representations of the sequence of operations in an information system or program. Information system flowcharts show how data from source documents flow through the computer to final distribution to users. Symbols used should be the internationally accepted standard. System flowcharts should be updated when necessary.

System Narratives: System narratives provide an overview explanation of system flowcharts, with key explanation of control points and system interfaces.

System Software: A collection of computer programs used in the design, processing, and control of all applications; the programs and processing routines that control the computer hardware; includes the operating system and utility programs.

Table Look-Ups: Used to assure that input data agree with predetermined criteria stored in a table.

Tape Management System (TMS): A system software tool that logs, monitors, and directs computer tape usage.

Telecommunications: Electronic communications by special devices over distances or around devices that preclude direct interpersonal exchange.

Teleprocessing : Using telecommunications facilities for handling and processing computerized information.

Terminal: A device for sending and receiving computerized data over transmission lines.

Terms-Alpha: Usually referring to the use of alphabetical character or character string, as opposed to numeric.

Test Data: Data that is used to test the programming logic of a test program. Test data may be created by a computer programmer or old unused production data depending on the use and purpose of the test.

Test Generators: Interactive debugging aids and code logic analyzers.

Test Programs: Programs that are tested and evaluated before approval into the production environment. Test programs, through a series of change control moves, migrate from the test environment to the production environment and become production programs.

Third Party Review: An independent audit of the control structure of a service organization, such as a service bureau, with the objective of providing assurances to the users of the service organization that the internal control structure is adequate, effective, and sound.

Token Ring Topology: A type of LAN ring topology in which a frame containing a specific format, called the token, is passed from one station to the next around the ring. When a station receives the token, it is allowed to transmit. The station can send as many frames as desired until a predefined time limit is reached. When a station either has no more frames to send or reaches the time limit, it transmits the token. Token passing prevents data collisions that can occur when two computers begin transmitting at the same time.

Topology: The physical layout of how computers are linked together. Examples include 'ring', 'star', and 'bus'.

Transaction: Business events or information grouped together because they have a single or similar purpose. Typically, a transaction is applied to a calculation or event that then results in the updating of a holding or master file.

Transaction Log: A manual or automated log of all updates to data files and databases.

Transmission Control Protocol/Internet Protocol (TCP/IP): A set of communications protocols that encompasses media access, packet transport, session communications, file transfer, electronic mail, terminal emulation, remote file access, and network management. TCP/IP provides the basis for the internet.

Trap Door: Unauthorized electronic exits or doorways out of an authorized computer program into a set of malicious instructions or programs.

Trojan Horse: Purposefully hidden malicious or damaging code within an authorized computer program.

Twisted Pairs: A pair of small insulated wires that are twisted around each other to minimize interfaces from other wires in the cable. This is a low-capacity transmission medium.

Uninterruptible Power Supply (UPS): Provides backup power for a computer system when the electrical power fails or drops to an unacceptable voltage level.

Unit Testing: Testing technique that is used to test program logic within a particular application or module. The purpose of the test is to ensure that the program meets system development guidelines and does not abend during processing.

Utility Programs: Specialized system software used to perform particular computerized functions and routines that are frequently required during normal processing. Examples include sorting, backup, and erasing of data.

Uploading: The process of electronically sending computerized information from a smaller computer to a larger one.

Vaccine: A program designed to detect computer viruses.

Validity Check: Programmed checking of data validity in accordance with predetermined criteria.

Value Added Network (VAN): A data communication network that adds processing services such as error correction, data, and/or storage to the basic function of transporting data.

Variable Sampling: A sampling technique used to estimate the average or total value of a population based on a sample.

Verification: Checks that data are entered correctly.

Virtual Private Network (VPN): A network that appears to be a single protected network behind firewalls, which actually encompasses encrypted virtual links over un-trusted networks.

Virtual Storage Access Method (VSAM): A system for accessing files stored on mass storage devices (disks). Used on IBM mainframes and plug-compatibles.

Virus: Malicious programs designed to spread and replicate from computer to computer through telecommunications links or through sharing of computer diskettes and files.

Voicemail: A system of storing messages in a private recording medium where the called party can later retrieve them.

Wide Area Network (WAN): A computer network connecting different remote locations that may range from short distances, such as a floor or building, to extremely long transmissions that encompass a large region or several countries.

Wiretapping: The fraudulent practice of eavesdropping on information being transmitted over telecommunications links.

X.25 Interface: Interface between data terminal equipment (DTE) and data circuit-terminating equipment (DCE) for terminals operating in the packet mode on public data networks.

Appendix B

CISA Sample Examination –
Choose Any 150 Questions

1. Which of the following most seriously compromises the independence of the internal auditing department?
   a) The director of internal auditing has dual reporting responsibility to the firm's top executive and the Audit Committee.
   b) Internal auditors frequently draft revised procedures for departments whose procedures they have criticized in an audit report.
   c) The internal auditing department and the firm's external auditors engage in joint planning of total audit coverage to avoid duplicating each other's work.
   d) The internal auditing department is included in the review cycle of the firm's contracts with other firms before the contracts are executed.
2. Database benefits from the auditor's viewpoint include the potential for:
   a) Consistency of data

b) Enhanced quality of audit by increased accessibility.

c) More accurate systems-development process.

d) Data resource management will accrue benefits through formalized discipline.

e) All of the above.

3. Major risks in online systems would include all of the following except:

a) Availability.

b) Late arrival of data.

c) Security.

d) Unauthorized access.

4. The type of processing where data is updated with immediate effect is known as:

a) Online.

b) Batch.

c) Transaction-based.

d) Real-time.

5. Which of the following would not normally be considered a typical file structure for a database management system?

a) Relational structure.

b) Hierarchical structure.

c) Network structure.

d) Batched sequential structure.

6. Communications unavailability can be controlled using all of the following except:

a) Adequate backups.

b) User authentication.

c) Peer-to-peer networking to permit mutual back-up.

d) Adequate Disaster Recovery Planning.

7. To trace data through several application programs, an auditor needs to know what programs use the data, which files contain the data, and which printed reports display the data. If data exists only in a database system, the auditor could probably find all of this information in a:

a) Data dictionary.

b) Database schema.

c) Data encryptor.

d) Decision table.

8. Which of the following is NOT true regarding upgrading software packages?
   a) Software upgrades to packages should be implemented via change control.
   b) All new releases of software packages should be acquired and implemented immediately.
   c) Software upgrades should be justified on the business needs.
   d) Software upgrades should be integrated into the overall business plans of the organization since they are designed to help the organization achieve its objectives.

9. Which of the following would NOT be considered an environmental control?
   a) Installation of a no-break power system.
   b) Logging of authorized and unauthorized attempts to access the computer area.
   c) Installation of a fire detection and extinguishing system.
   d) Validation of passwords and transaction codes by the access control software.

10. An electronics firm has decided to acquire a new application system by purchasing a package. Which of the following would NOT be included in the evaluation of alternative systems?
    a) Whether the system will run in a client-server environment.
    b) Type of database and file structures used.
    c) Compatibility with existing systems.
    d) Number of sites where successful implementation has occurred.

11. Acceptable business reasons to undertake a business change process would include all of the reasons below EXCEPT:
    a) Elimination of competitive disadvantage.
    b) Creating a business breakthrough.
    c) Compatibility with existing systems.
    d) Corporate survival.

12. Critical success factors in controlling a business process change project would include all of the following except:
    a) Ensuring the re-engineering is appropriate.
    b) Understanding the business processes.

c) Appointing the right leader.

d) Speed of change.

13. A common reason for the failure of business process change projects would be:

    a) Over-optimistic timescales.

    b) The transformation is not owned by the implementers at the user end.

    c) Inadequately trained staff.

    d) Radical changes to the business itself.

14. Critical success factors in implementing and maintaining acquired software would include:

    a) There is a quality education and training program.

    b) Policies and procedures relating to compliance with external requirements have been documented and communicated.

    c) Job rotation for career development is implemented.

    d) A feedback mechanism is implemented for optimizing and continuously improving the process.

15. Key indicators that a business process change project has been successful would include all of the following EXCEPT:

    a) Number of findings during the quality assurance review of installation and accreditation functions.

    b) Degree of stakeholder satisfaction with the new process.

    c) Degree of seamlessness of integration into existing business processes.

    d) Degree of achievement of cost reduction and operational effectiveness objectives.

16. Which of the following is not one of the three types of access controls?

    a) Administrative.

    b) Personnel.

    c) Technical.

    d) Physical.

17. Which of the following is the strongest form of authentication?

    a) Something you know.

    b) Something you are.

    c) Passwords.

    d) Tokens.

18. In which one of the following documents is the assignment of individual roles and responsibilities MOST appropriately defined?
    a) Security policy.
    b) Enforcement guidelines.
    c) Acceptable use policy.
    d) Program manual
19. Which of the following is not part of physical access control?
    a) CCTV.
    b) Man-traps.
    c) Data classification and labeling.
    d) Biometrics.
20. Factors that should be considered when evaluating audit risk in an IS functional area include:
    1. Volume of transactions.
    2. Degree of system integration.
    3. Years since last audit.
    4. Significant management turnover.
    5. Value of 'assets at risk'.
    6. Average value per transaction.
    7. Results of last audit.

    Factors that best define materiality of audit risk are:
    a) 1 through 7.
    b) 2, 4, and 7.
    c) 1, 5, and 6.
    d) 3, 4, and 6.
21. Which of the following audit steps would an IS auditor normally perform FIRST when conducting a review of hardware acquisition procedures?
    a) Testing compliance to management directives.
    b) Determine the adequacy of the hardware for the intended task.
    c) Determining the management directives that pertain to hardware acquisition.
    d) Observing the purchasing procedure for proper segregation of duties.
22. Corporate IT governance is the responsibility of:
    a) The board and management.

    b) The IS manager.

    c) The IS auditor.

    d) The audit committee.

23. Organizations develop change control procedures to ensure that:

    a) Changes are controlled by the Change Controller.

    b) All changes are requested, scheduled, and completed on time.

    c) All changes are authorized, tested, and recorded.

    d) Management is advised of changes made to system.

24. Control problems during business process change would typically include:

    a) Poor control over file conversions.

    b) Changing effectiveness of existing control structures.

    c) Employee uncertainty and lack of co-operation.

    d) Changing control objectives.

25. Which one of the following statements describes management controls?

    a) They prevent users from accessing any control function.

    b) They eliminate the need for most auditing functions.

    c) They are generally inexpensive to implement.

    d) They may be administrative, procedural, or technical.

26. A common security issue that is extremely hard to control in large environments occurs when a user has more computer rights, permissions, and privileges than required for the tasks the user needs to fulfill. This is an example of:

    a) Excessive Rights.

    b) Excessive Access.

    c) Excessive Privileges.

    d) Excessive Permissions.

27. According to Sarbanes-Oxley, management's report on internal control over financial reporting is required to include:

    a) A statement of the IT manager's responsibility for establishing and maintaining adequate internal control over financial reporting for the company.

    b) A statement identifying the framework used by management to conduct a required assessment of the effectiveness of the company's internal control over financial reporting strategic process.

    c) The use of COBIT® as a control framework for evaluating internal controls.

    d) The use of professional IT auditors.

28. Risk is commonly expressed as a function of the:

    a) Systems vulnerabilities and the cost to mitigate.

    b) Likelihood that the harm will occur and its potential impact.

    c) Types of countermeasures needed and the system's vulnerabilities.

    d) Computer system-related assets and their costs.

29. The primary reason for an IS risk-based audit approach is:

    a) To control costs within the IS function.

    b) To show management the areas in which the controls are deficient.

    c) To show the audit committee that IS audit is being carried out in an appropriate manner.

    d) To permit the efficient allocation of limited IS audit resources.

30. Need-to-know is defined as:

    a) Access to, or possession of information based on need to perform security duties.

    b) Possession of information based on need to perform assigned duties.

    c) Access to, or possession of information based on need to perform assigned job duties.

    d) Knowledge of information or activities based on need to perform job functions.

31. The starting point for risk-based audit approach is:

    a) Determination of the overall business objectives of the organization.

    b) Determination of the individual detailed control objectives.

    c) Identification of the internal controls relied upon by management.

    d) Identification of best practice in selecting internal controls.

32. Discretionary audit activities are those activities which:

    a) Must be carried out within the timespan of the audit plan.

    b) Are based upon management's requests.

    c) Are decided upon using only the most important risk factors.

    d) Are decided upon using all risk factors.

33. Which one of the following is a core infrastructure and service element of Business Continuity Planning (BCP)?

    a) The risk management process.

    b) Internal and external support functions.

    c) The change management process.

    d) Backup and restoration functions.

34. Deliverables from a risk assessment process are threats identified, controls selected, action plan complete, and:

    a) Risk level established.

    b) Technical issues quantified.

    c) Vulnerability assessment completed.

    d) Risk mitigation established.

35. Which of the following statements is true about risks?

    a) When evaluating risks their impact should be considered, however probability of occurrence is not important.

    b) Risks if they happen always have negative impact and not positive.

    c) The risks may be documented in detail in a Risk Register.

    d) The Risk Register is another name for Risk Management Plan.

36. A charter is being drafted for a newly formed IT audit activity. Which of these would be the most appropriate organizational status to be incorporated into the charter?

    a) The chief IT audit executive should report to the chief executive officer but have access to the audit committee.

    b) The chief IT audit executive should be a member of the audit committee of the board of directors.

    c) The chief IT audit executive should report to the chief financial officer.

    d) The chief IT audit executive should report to the chief information officer.

37. One of the biggest barriers to achieving effective auditing in an IT environment is:

    a) Lack of appropriate IT audit skills.

    b) The assumption that IT audit is a separate, unique, and special audit discipline.

    c) Lack of availability of CAATs.

    d) Overemphasis on accounting and general business auditing.

38. The IT audit executive should develop and maintain a quality assurance and improvement program that covers all aspects of the IT audit activity and continuously monitors its effectiveness with all of the following included except:

    a) Periodic internal assessment.

    b) Annual appraisals of individual internal auditors' performance.

    c) Supervision.

    d) Periodic external assessments.

39. The IT Audit Charter should include:

    a) Mission and scope of work.

    b) Independence.

    c) Accountability.

    d) All of the above.

40. An advantage of a centralized IS audit function is:

    a) Close ties at local level.

    b) Use of a non-standardized audit approach.

    c) Independence from local management.

    d) The auditor may be seen as an outsider.

41. The audit program provides for the collection of audit evidence of:

    a) Structures.

    b) Documentation standards.

    c) Systems documentation.

    d) All of the above.

42. Project control is primarily designed to:

    a) Maximize the likelihood of successful outcomes.

    b) Eliminate delivery risk.

    c) Minimize the risk of non-achievement of objectives.

    d) Control the consumption of resources.

43. Key indicators that system change project has been successful would include all of the following EXCEPT:

    a) Number of findings during the quality assurance review of installation and accreditation functions.

    b) Degree of stakeholder satisfaction with the new process.

    c) Degree of seamlessness of integration into existing business processes.

    d) Degree of achievement of cost reduction and operational effectiveness objectives.

44. Critical success factors in implementing and maintaining acquired software would include:

    a) There is a quality education and training program.

    b) Policies and procedures relating to compliance with external requirements have been documented and communicated.

    c) Job rotation for career development is implemented.

    d) A feedback mechanism is implemented for optimizing and continuously improving the process.

45. An electronics firm has decided to acquire a new application system by purchasing a package. Which of the following would NOT be included in the evaluation of alternative systems?

    a) Whether the system will run in a client-server environment.

    b) Type of database and file structures used.

    c) Compatibility with existing systems.

    d) Number of sites where successful implementation has occurred.

46. Information processing facility operations include all except:

    a) Mounting and dismounting data files.

    b) Loading paper into printers.

    c) Writing computer programs.

    d) Scheduling runs.

47. In evaluating the planning aspects, audit would typically look at all except:

    a) Management's forecasting of needs and requirements.

    b) Management's delivery of goals.

    c) Management's devising of strategies.

    d) Management's development of policies.

48. The Chief IT Auditor has received the following from the president of the organization: 'You are directed to discontinue any further investigation in this audit until informed by me to proceed'. The Chief IT Auditor should:

    a) Immediately report the communication to The Institute of Internal Auditors and ask for an ethical interpretation and guidance.

b) Continue to investigate the area until all the facts are determined and document all the relevant facts in the engagement records.

c) Immediately notify the external auditors of the problem to avoid aiding and abetting a potential crime by the organization.

d) Inform the president that this scope limitation will need to be reported to the board and the audit committee.

49. Fraud typically involves:
   a) Actual prejudice.
   b) Use of the Internet.
   c) Intentional misrepresentation.
   d) Loss of confidentiality.

50. The main difference between governance and management is that management is involved with everything except:
   a) Achieving the current and future needs of the organization in a controlled manner.
   b) Ensuring the ongoing supply of quality services and products.
   c) Controlling costs.
   d) Ensuring continuous feedback mechanisms for the measurement of performance.

51. PCI DSS standards include:
   a) Changing vendor supplied defaults for system passwords.
   b) Detecting stored cardholder data.
   c) Use of regularly updated antivirus software.
   d) All of the above.

52. Electronic eavesdropping involves:
   a) Obtaining information from wastebaskets.
   b) Use of the internet.
   c) Interception of a communication.
   d) Use of a computer.

53. Legislation requires annual affirmation of management's responsibility for internal controls over financial reporting. Management must attest to effectiveness based on an evaluation and the auditor must attest and report on management's evaluation. This legislation is known as:
   a) Foreign Corrupt Practices Act.

b) Model Business Corporation Act.

c) Sarbanes–Oxley.

d) Gramm–Leach–Bliley Act.

54. The COBIT® toolset also includes provisions for all of the following except:

a) Maturity models for assessing your organization's control over processes in comparison with industry and international standards.

b) Critical success factors defining the most important implementation guidelines.

c) Specification of Data Encryption standards.

d) Key performance indicators that define measures that communicate to management whether the IT processes have met their business requirements.

55. Factors to consider when assessing independence on an ongoing basis throughout an audit engagement include all of the following except:

a) Previous work done in this area.

b) The financial interests of the auditor.

c) Opportunities for personal advantage or financial gain.

d) Prior work assignments and responsibilities.

56. COSO defined the objectives that all businesses strive for to include:

a) Economy and efficiency of operations, including achievement of performance goals and safeguarding of assets against loss.

b) Reliable financial and operational data and reports.

c) Compliance with laws and regulations.

d) All of the above.

57. ISO 27002 includes among its component areas all of the following except:

a) Organization of Information Security.

b) Management authority levels.

c) Human Resources Security.

d) Physical Security.

58. Among the five components defined by COSO were all except:

a) A sound control environment.

b) A sound risk-assessment process.

c) Effective management procedures.

d) Sound information and communications systems.

e) Effective monitoring.

59. In a change control environment, the assurance of proper changes to source programs in production status is increased by all of the following except:

a) Programmer access.

b) Authorization of the change.

c) Testing of the change.

d) Documentation of the change.

60. Because of their portable nature, tablet computers:

a) Do not require change control.

b) Require the same change control procedures as mainframes.

c) May require different change control procedures.

d) Require only problem management procedures.

61. A performance management measures which aspects of the organization?

a) How well the business needs are matched with the deliverables.

b) what processes are in place to track and communicate the performance.

c) How effective the mechanisms are to correct or escalate situations that are out of the acceptable boundaries of performance.

d) All of the above.

62. Operational auditing involves assessing the quality of controls leading to:

a) Effectiveness.

b) Efficiency.

c) Economy.

d) All of the above.

63. The final step in the change control process is:

a) Validated and approved.

b) Report change to management.

c) Test and implement.

d) Review and approve.

64. In order to determine the overall management governance in place, the auditor may examine:
    a) Management's measurement of the workload.
    b) Capacity measuring and measurement against standards.
    c) Customer satisfaction.
    d) Management's attainment of agreed service levels.
    e) All of the above.

65. Program change controls are intended to ensure that all changes are:
    a) Audited to verify intent.
    b) Implemented into production systems.
    c) Within established performance criteria.
    d) Tested to ensure correctness.

66. Performance measurement systems are designed to:
    a) Prove compliance with COBIT®.
    b) Provide a balanced, methodical method of assessing the effectiveness of an organization's operations.
    c) Provide feedback on costs.
    d) Ensure best practice is implemented.

67. A prerequisite for an effective operational audit is the existence of:
    a) Measurable standards.
    b) Strong internal controls.
    c) Implementation of COSO.
    d) All of the above.

68. The primary causes of development exposures include:
    a) Violation of legal statutes.
    b) Excessive operating cost.
    c) Poor communications.
    d) Inflexibility.

69. Benefits of e-business include all of the following except:
    a) A more effective delivery of existing goods and services.
    b) Providing products and services that did not exist prior to the advent of the internet.
    c) The creation of new business ideas involving the generation of a new set of services.
    d) Delivery of hard products from a portfolio available to the organization.

70. CCM contributes value to risk management and compliance initiatives in ways including:
    a) Improving operational performance.
    b) Reducing financial governance.
    c) Increasing manual sampling.
    d) Reducing the availability of working capital.

71. The Continuous Monitoring process includes all except:
    a) Categorization of Information System.
    b) Increasing of Security Controls.
    c) Assessment of Security Controls.
    d) Authorization of Information Systems.

72. Major causes of program maintenance may include all except:
    a) Bugs or errors in the program.
    b) The age of the system.
    c) Corporate mergers and acquisitions.
    d) Governmental regulations that require changes in the program.

73. In the SDLC, user specifications include:
    a) File and record layouts.
    b) Operational constraints.
    c) Assignments of responsibility.
    d) Access rules.

74. In the SDLC, Implementation typically involves:
    a) Prototyping.
    b) Operational constraints.
    c) Assignments of responsibility.
    d) Access rules.

75. SDLC consists of a finite and predefined number of tasks, which include all except:
    a) Audit.
    b) Interpret.
    c) Code.
    d) Test.

76. Reasons for systems failure may include:
    a) Poor staff attitude.
    b) Management over-controlling.
    c) Too many business objectives.
    d) Too many user requirements specified.

77. Change control involves ensuring:
    a) All changes are authorized.
    b) All authorized changes are made.
    c) Only authorized changes are made.
    d) All of the above.
78. The conversion phase of the SDLC typically involves:
    a) Documentation.
    b) Parallel running.
    c) User training.
    d) Sanitization of input data.
79. Factors to be considered in conducting systems reviews include:
    a) Mission.
    b) Goals and objectives.
    c) Procedures.
    d) All of the above.
80. Sanitization of input data is a common requirement within:
    a) Installation.
    b) Testing.
    c) Conversion activities.
    d) Change control.
81. The SAS 70 reports which cover both the description and opinion as well as the results of the independent service auditor's tests to measure effectiveness of the control structures is a:
    a) Type 1 Report.
    b) Type 2 Report.
    c) None of the above.
    d) All of the above.
82. Major causes of program maintenance include:
    a) Changes to procedures.
    b) Reliability.
    c) Corporate mergers and acquisitions.
    d) Response time.
83. Disadvantages of acquiring purchased packages include:
    a) Higher initial costs.
    b) Less risk.
    c) Low quality.
    d) More time.

84. Systems acquisition may require purchasing, leasing, or renting computer resources from an IT vendor, which could include:
    a) Computer dealers and distributors.
    b) Leasing companies.
    c) Time-sharing companies.
    d) All of the above.

85. The make-or-buy decision for systems acquisition is made depending on a variety of criteria including:
    a) Time constraints.
    b) User knowledge.
    c) Supplier relationship.
    d) Supplier support.

86. Which of these situations may require the development of new systems?
    a) Acquisition of a new organization.
    b) New government reporting requirements.
    c) Improved departmental efficiency.
    d) All of the above.

87. A finding of the feasibility study not to proceed with any systems development or acquisition may be seen as:
    a) An acceptable finding.
    b) An unacceptable finding.
    c) An expected finding.
    d) An unexpected finding.

88. Where inadequate details have been included regarding the planning, control, and project management of the system, the auditor must:
    a) Draw this to management's attention.
    b) Report this in an interim report.
    c) Report this in the final report.
    d) All of the above.

89. The typical structure of a feasibility study would normally include:
    a) The service delivery requirements and impacts on existing IT processing as well as other user functional areas.
    b) Business disruptions anticipated as a result of the development, conversion, and implementation process including the acquisition or training of staff within the user area.

    c) Evaluation criteria used to select among alternatives.

    d) All of the above.

90. Factors to be considered in conducting a feasibility study include:

    a) The programming language the new system.

    b) The likelihood of successful implementation.

    c) The extent of documentation required.

    d) The number of sites running a package.

91. Where an in-house developed solution is decided upon, the feasibility study should include sections on:

    a) Overview of the proposed system in business functionality terms.

    b) Technological alternatives considered together with the cost benefit analysis of each.

    c) Analysis of the alternative courses of actions compared to the selection criteria.

    d) All of the above.

92. In order that ongoing monitoring and project control can be effected, budgets must be complete and structured in detail for:

    a) Management.

    b) Hardware.

    c) Cost.

    d) Planning.

93. Included within the feasibility study should be a section on:

    a) The use of the 'waterfall' methodology for the SDLC.

    b) The availability of resources to carry out the appropriate development or implementation.

    c) The detailed system specification.

    d) The access controls required for the new system.

94. Where an in-house developed solution is decided upon, the feasibility study should include sections on:

    a) Analysis of the costs and benefits associated with each alternative.

    b) Operational, security, and control risks associated with each alternative together with the control structures considered for risk minimization of each.

    c) Availability of resources internally and externally to carry out the appropriate development or implementation.

    d) All of the above.

95. Data conversion and acquisition must ensure:
    a) Programs to convert data from old systems have been developed appropriately.
    b) Valid date has been converted accurately and completely.
    c) Conversion routines have been fully tested.
    d) All data has been re-loaded from scratch.

96. One of the common problems in using source code review is:
    a) The difficulty of ensuring that the program reviewed is the live program.
    b) The auditor may be biased in the selection of the coding to be reviewed.
    c) The live system may be corrupted.
    d) Disclosure of data may occur.

97. The technique of taking a known transaction and following through the processing cycle in order to check the processing logic of a program is a technique known as:
    a) Sampling.
    b) Integrated test facility.
    c) Test data.
    d) Snapshot technique.

98. A technique used to determine the accuracy and completeness of processing by reprocessing live data through a program which is not the live program is an audit technique known as:
    a) Parallel simulation.
    b) Integrated test facility.
    c) Test data.
    d) Snapshot technique.

99. Processing the auditor's transactions along with live data to transact against a dummy department is a technique known as:
    a) Test data.
    b) Integrated test facility.
    c) Source code review.
    d) Snapshot technique.

100. Input control objectives at the input stage would include all of the following except:
    a) All transactions are initially and completely recorded.
    b) All transactions are completely and accurately entered into the system.

  c) All rejected transactions are reported, corrected, and re-input.

  d) All transactions are entered only once.

101. Appropriate controls over inputs may include:
  a) Data validation.
  b) Control totals.
  c) Programmed balancing.
  d) Restricted access.

102. Appropriate controls over processing may include:
  a) Data validation.
  b) Activity logging.
  c) Document scanning.
  d) Programmed balancing.

103. Common problems the auditor will encounter in running CAATs include all of the following except:
  a) Getting the wrong files.
  b) Getting the wrong layout.
  c) Documentation is out of date.
  d) Working with printouts.

104. Characteristics of good systems include all of the following attributes except:
  a) Relevance.
  b) Simplicity.
  c) Frequency.
  d) Timeliness.

105. In the absence of continuous auditing, the auditor can still gain satisfaction as to the adequacy of controls over the infrastructure by ensuring that management:
  a) Enforces the use of standardized administrator passwords.
  b) Maintains an activity audit trail with real-time monitoring.
  c) Bans all infrastructure changes.
  d) Bans all changes to application programs.

106. Effective configuration management requires knowledge of all of the following except:
  a) Location and identification of all components.
  b) Status and release levels of all software.
  c) Accuracy and completeness of all component information.
  d) Proper authorization procedures for acquisition.

107. Key controls around the risks inherent in the changing of the IT infrastructure due to ongoing development or maintenance would include:
    a) Employment of only IT continuity plans in order to ensure that critical operations continue to be available during any period of disruption.
    b) Implementation of specialized controls surrounding the management and life cycle of IT assets.
    c) Up-to-date definition of the roles and responsibilities for the management of IT infrastructure assets.
    d) Using only IT infrastructure equipment and services that do not require effective approval and certification of new technology to meet operational requirements.

108. Network components include all of the following except:
    a) Communications equipment.
    b) Services rendered to provide networks.
    c) Utility software.
    d) Network-related software.

109. In reviewing the IT infrastructure, the IT auditor would review all of the following aspects except:
    a) Corporate technology standards.
    b) User access controls.
    c) Overall IT architecture governance.
    d) IT infrastructure investment management.

110. Conducting a security review in today's environment is a complex operation involving all of the following except:
    a) The SDLC.
    b) Firewall rules.
    c) Server privilege settings.
    d) Authentication procedures.

111. Continuous monitoring would normally be used to ensure all of the following except:
    a) No system offers full access permissions to anonymous Logins.
    b) Online availability is appropriately maintained.
    c) No changes are made to individuals authorized to have specific levels of access into live databases.
    d) No unauthorized changes are made to access control lists.

112. Cost aspects within the Service Center include:
    a) Cost of quality.
    b) Appraisal costs.
    c) Internal failure costs.
    d) All of the above.

113. Service Level Agreements are the formal document specifying:
    a) The performance criteria.
    b) Security levels agreed.
    c) Cost structures to be applied in delivery of service.
    d) All of the above.

114. Service center problems commonly occur when:
    a) Changes are not regularly made.
    b) System components are upgraded.
    c) Failure occurs only in a single component.
    d) Versions of operating systems never change.

115. Changes within the service center can be:
    a) Triggered by failure of infrastructure.
    b) Triggered by the desire to maintain infrastructure.
    c) Hardware-based only.
    d) Software-based only.

116. Evaluating systems availability includes evaluating all of the following except:
    a) System resilience.
    b) Ability to withstand security breaches.
    c) Cost of system non-availability.
    d) Ease of system recovery.

117. An adequate security architecture would include elements of:
    a) Workstation security.
    b) Encryption.
    c) Segregation of duties.
    d) All of the above.

118. Computer Security myths include:
    a) Computer Security is a technical problem.
    b) Computer Security is the responsibility of all the employees.
    c) Computer Security cannot be attained.
    d) Computer Security takes considerable corporate effort and resources.

119. Data integrity being undermined by inadequacy some security is an example of:
    a) A technical concern.
    b) A business concern.
    c) Both the technical and business concern.
    d) Neither a technical nor a business concern.

120. The business impact of a failure of Computer Security may include:
    a) Authorized employees proving to be risk agents.
    b) Computer facilities may be subject to damage by disgruntled employees.
    c) Accounting and financial records may be falsified.
    d) All of the above.

121. Encryption does not prevent:
    a) Message destruction.
    b) Message inaccuracy.
    c) Lack of timeliness of message delivery.
    d) All of the above.

122. The integrity of transmitted messages can be assisted by all of the following except:
    a) Steganography.
    b) Message if integration codes.
    c) Public key cryptography.
    d) Double public key cryptography.

123. The scope of Computer Security includes all of the following except:
    a) Systems software security.
    b) Telecommunications availability.
    c) Vital records retention.
    d) IS insurance.

124. Passwords should be all of the following except:
    a) Hard to guess.
    b) Easy to remember.
    c) Written down.
    d) Frequently changed.

125. Top Secrets nodes include all of the following except:
    a) Dormant.
    b) Abort.

c) Warn.

d) Fail.

126. Systems specifically designed as Security Software include all except:

a) LIBRARIAN.

b) RACF.

c) Top Secret.

d) ACF2.

127. Common operating environment security parameters include all of the following except:

a) Password rules.

b) The event logging parameters.

c) Encryption.

d) Login time restrictions.

128. In auditing that computing operational environment, the auditor can still look for normal controls such as:

a) Segregation duties.

b) Organization work.

c) Appropriate supervision.

d) All of the above.

129. Client server is an architecture in which the functionality and processing of a system are split between:

a) The client workstation and a database server.

b) The client workstation and a mainframe.

c) The client workstation and the internet.

d) The client workstation and the rest of the network.

130. A digital signature uses similar technology to:

a) Symmetric encryption.

b) MACing.

c) Asymmetric encryption.

d) None of the above.

131. A firewall provides an organization with:

a) A mechanism for implementing and enforcing network access security policies.

b) A transformation of directive of discretionary controls into preventative controls.

c) Control over access to and from a given network.

d) All of the above.

132. The distribution of functionality in client-server systems causes the vulnerability of the systems to viruses, fraud, and misuse to:
    a) Decrease.
    b) Increase.
    c) Double.
    d) Stay the same.

133. Networks are genetically seen as vulnerable in the area of:
    a) The interception of data.
    b) Unauthorized access.
    c) Availability of communications.
    d) All of the above.

134. Network areas containing information resources which are open to a restricted number of authorized users who are identified and authenticated would be seen as:
    a) Untrusted zones.
    b) Trusted zones.
    c) Semi-trusted zones.
    d) Hostile zones.

135. Common risks organizations may face from failures of Network Security include all except:
    a) Loss of staff.
    b) Loss of reputation.
    c) Loss of confidentiality.
    d) System unavailability.

136. Structural collapse of office buildings containing Computer Centers can be caused by:
    a) Earth tremors.
    b) Poorly built structures.
    c) Impacts at ground level.
    d) All of the above.

137. For fire to catch hold it requires a plentiful supply of:
    a) Oxygen.
    b) Heat.
    c) Fuel source.
    d) All of the above.

138. Physical risks include all of the following except:
    a) Unauthorized use of passwords.
    b) Theft of equipment.

    c) Loss of data confidentiality.

    d) Destruction of hardware.

139. Shredders may be used to ensure confidential scrap is not made available to unauthorized sources including the shredding of:

    a) DVDs.

    b) Microfiche.

    c) Paper.

    d) All of the above.

140. Controls over physical access may include all of the following except:

    a) Fences and walls.

    b) Encryption.

    c) Locks on doors.

    d) Formal identification cards.

141. Physical security encompasses control measures to mitigate the risks of natural events including all of the following except:

    a) Flood.

    b) Earthquake.

    c) Fire.

    d) Tsunami.

142. Where a disaster would result in conspicuous interruption of IT Services, potentially result in loss of business, disaster preparedness would typically be classified as:

    a) Poor.

    b) Weak.

    c) Adequate.

    d) Good.

143. In classifying systems recovery by degrees of priority, priorities may include all of the following except:

    a) Importance to the Board of Directors.

    b) Alternative service level required.

    c) Business lost rating.

    d) Maximum tolerable downtime.

144. A commonly omitted consideration in the development of a recovery plan is a provision of alternatives for:

    a) Hardware.

b) Communications.

c) Stationery supplies.

d) Air conditioning.

145. Threats which could trigger the use of the disaster recovery plan include:

a) Industrial action.

b) Viruses.

c) Terrorism.

d) All of the above.

146. The business continuity plan will require elements addressing the organizational risks and will typically include sections on all of the following except:

a) Contracting with vendors.

b) Email.

c) Fire.

d) Acceptable use.

147. A 'hot' site is seen to be one in which instant availability exists for all of the following except:

a) Hardware.

b) Communications capability.

c) Systems software.

d) Current data.

148. In conducting an audit of the contingency plan, the auditor will seek evidence of all of the following except:

a) The adequacy of the plan.

b) The effectiveness of the implementation of the plan.

c) The input of Audit in developing the plan.

d) The existence of a mechanism for keeping the plan up to date and relevant.

149. In satisfying himself that the contingency plan will be kept up to date and appropriate, the auditor will typically ensure all of the following except:

a) The master plan is kept secure.

b) Executive management is involved in the maintenance of the plan.

c) Distributed copies of kept up to date and secure.

d) The responsibility for planned maintenance has been properly assigned.

150. Should disruption occur, the consequences could include any or all of the following except:
    a) Increased efficiency.
    b) Loss of revenues.
    c) Incurred costs.
    d) Loss of discounts.

151. Insurance can be sought for all of the following except:
    a) Maintenance costs.
    b) Mechanical breakdown.
    c) Fraud and dishonesty.
    d) Civil unrest.

152. Risks specific to portable computers include all of the following except:
    a) Accidental damage in transit.
    b) Ease of theft.
    c) Unauthorized access.
    d) Lost in transit.

153. Where unauthorized access to an organization's Computer Systems has resulted in a breach of privacy legislation, civil or criminal action against the organization can involve:
    a) Fines.
    b) Penalties.
    c) Consequential damages.
    d) All of the above.

154. Typical external attacks on Computer Systems may include all of the following except:
    a) Outside penetration of secured systems.
    b) Insider financial fraud.
    c) Data Network sabotage.
    d) Denial of service attacks.

155. In terms of risk management, risks are usually divided into:
    a) Those risks that are appropriate to control.
    b) Those risks that cannot be avoided and must be accepted.
    c) Those risks which remain unacceptable and can be transferred to third parties.
    d) All of the above.

156. In EDI contracts, terms and conditions typically include all of the following except:
    a) Quality of goods to be supplied.
    b) Which laws will govern.
    c) When is a contract 'received'.
    d) What is the definition of a signature.

157. Fraud within e-commerce may involve:
    a) Invalid contracts.
    b) Suppliers not being paid for goods and services delivered.
    c) Agencies not receiving services/goods already paid for.
    d) All of the above.

158. Benefits of successful E-commerce implementation include all of the following except:
    a) Reduced transaction costs and greater productivity.
    b) Service availability 24 hours a day, 7 days a week.
    c) Reduced transportation costs.
    d) Opportunities for local business to grow and compete in the global marketplace.

159. For e-commerce to be successful, information must be available to other participants in the trading community. This can put information at risk including all of the following except:
    a) Cost structures.
    b) Individuals' private information.
    c) Information on discounts offered.
    d) Products and services available.

160. Anticipated benefits of EDI include:
    a) Improved control of data.
    b) Decreased administrative costs.
    c) All of the above.
    d) None of the above.

161. Corruption of data within an e-commerce system could result in:
    a) Destruction of the audit trail.
    b) Loss of confidentiality.
    c) Disclosure of cost structures.
    d) Disclosure of conditions and services offered to other customers.

162. In order to function effectively, EDI requires all of the following except:
    a) A standard format of a common language used between trading partners.
    b) Symmetrical encryption.
    c) Translation software performing file conversions to and from standard formats.
    d) A data communication link.

163. Known password weaknesses include:
    a) No password required.
    b) Poor change control.
    c) Poor personnel policies.
    d) All of the above.

164. Hacker threats in the cloud environment can arise in any cloud service except:
    a) SaaS.
    b) QaaS.
    c) DaaS.
    d) IaaS.

165. Robust approaches to logical information security include the use of all of the following except:
    a) Use of biometrics.
    b) One-time passwords.
    c) Compartmentalization of accesses and privileges.
    d) Hardening of operating systems.

166. Browser-based attacks include all of the following techniques except:
    a) Phishing.
    b) Botnets.
    c) Zombie computers.
    d) Cross-site scripting.

167. Hackers tools to gain access to passwords include all of the following except:
    a) Password guessers.
    b) War-dialers.
    c) Adware.
    d) Key loggers.

168. Hackers may gain user-IDs by any of the following except:
    a) Trying the standard user-IDs that come with a system.
    b) Straightforward trial and error.
    c) Insider information on the installation.
    d) Copying the password file.

169. Tasks of the incident response team may include all of the following except:
    a) Assess the damage and scope.
    b) Maintain their own anonymity.
    c) Maintain a chain of custody.
    d) Protect privacy rights.

170. Evidence to be sought in investigating an incident may include:
    a) Listing of files accessed.
    b) Email sent and received.
    c) Programs executed.
    d) All of the above.

171. Failure of successful prosecution can be as a result of any of the following except:
    a) Evidence which is not legally gathered.
    b) Evidence extracted directly from the Computer System.
    c) Evidence where the chain of custody has not been correctly maintained.
    d) Evidence which is inconclusive.

172. An incident response methodology should include all of the following except:
    a) Effective use of biometrics.
    b) Detection of incidents.
    c) Response strategy formulation.
    d) Forensic duplication.

173. Major steps in pre-incident preparation would include:
    a) Identifying the vital assets in advance.
    b) Determining the most likely nature of exposure faced.
    c) Producing cryptographic checksums of critical files.
    d) All of the above.

174. Standard hardware tools for forensic investigation could include any of the following except:
    a) 2 to 3 native operating systems.

b) Burn Bags.

c) Digital camera.

d) Lockable evidence storage containers.

175. An appropriate user response to an attempted fraud could be any of the following except:

a) Ignore the incident.

b) Defend against further attacks.

c) Prosecute all cases.

d) Gather data of the incident for future use.

Appendix C

Sample Examination Answers

1. B	20. A	39. D	58. C	77. D
2. E	21. C	40. C	59. A	78. D
3. B	22. A	41. D	60. C	79. D
4. D	23. C	42. C	61. D	80. C
5. D	24. A	43. A	62. D	81. B
6. B	25. D	44. D	63. B	82. C
7. B	26. C	45. A	64. E	83. A
8. B	27. B	46. C	65. D	84. D
9. D	28. B	47. B	66. B	85. A
10. A	29. D	48. D	67. A	86. D
11. C	30. C	49. C	68. C	87. A
12. A	31. A	50. A	69. D	88. C
13. B	32. C	51. D	70. A	89. B
14. D	33. A	52. C	71. B	90. B
15. A	34. A	53. C	72. B	91. D
16. B	35. B	54. C	73. C	92. D
17. B	36. A	55. A	74. A	93. C
18. C	37. B	56. D	75. B	94. D
19. C	38. D	57. B	76. A	95. A

96. A	112. D	128. D	144. C	160. C
97. D	113. D	129. A	145. D	161. A
98. A	114. B	130. C	146. B	162. B
99. B	115. A	131. D	147. D	163. D
100. C	116. C	132. B	148. C	164. B
101. A	117. D	133. D	149. B	165. A
102. D	118. A	134. C	150. A	166. A
103. D	119. B	135. A	151. A	167. B
104. C	120. D	136. D	152. C	168. D
105. D	121. D	137. D	153. D	169. B
106. B	122. A	138. A	154. B	170. D
107. C	123. B	139. D	155. D	171. B
108. C	124. C	140. B	156. A	172. A
109. B	125. B	141. C	157. D	173. D
110. A	126. A	142. B	158. C	174. A
111. B	127. C	143. A	159. D	175. A

Index